Strong Roots
Have No Fear

EMPOWERING CHILDREN TO THRIVE IN A
MULTICULTURAL WORLD WITH INTUITIVE PARENTING

Aditi Wardhan Singh

© 2019 Aditi Wardhan Singh

Raising World Children LLC

ISBN-13: 978-1-7335649-0-8

I would love to hear about your experiences with multicultural living. Every voice and story matters in the conversation for empowering the next generation. Feel free to email the RWC Team with your stories and questions at contact@raisingworldchildren.com

The **FREE** companion items to this book including effective parenting resources, easy to use check lists, teaching materials, handouts and more can be found here to motivate your children towards an empowered, multicultural mindset curious to learn about the world.
RaisingWorldChildren.com

For testimonials by parents around the world about the work done by Aditi Wardhan Singh, visit -
StrongRootsBook.com

DEDICATION

*"Give the ones you love wings to fly,
roots to come back and reasons to stay."*

- Dalai Lama

For my two magical stars. My inspiration.

You and your friends, the children of the world are my hope
for an enlightened future. May your sparkles spread to every
life you touch, much like the glitter you craft with. May you
take on life empowered with the wisdom of yesterdays and an
awareness of your todays. With a true knowledge of yourself,
stand confident, constantly doing your part in standing strong
in an ever-evolving world.

Remember, your home and family are wherever your heart is.

CONTENTS

ACKNOWLEDGMENTS

Ma, Daddy
Your life lessons are ingrained in me. The ones you taught me, the ones you imparted by example and even the ones you did not know to. Thank You for shaping my past so I could look towards my present with content and future with aspiration.

Hubby dearest
Nothing would be possible without you taking care of the kids while I penned down my days and learnings. You pushed me to become a writer and rooted for me when I had the colossal idea of bringing parents from around the world together. You are the rudder of my ship, keeping me to true to my desire for a unified world. Thank you for all you do.
Thank you for being You!

My Friends
Few people in the world are as blessed as me with the amazing support system that encouraged me by cheering every milestone I achieved. Tracy Mathew, you gave me my first journal 20 years ago and that kept me writing. Parul Agarwal, you inspire me to follow my dreams.
My heart overflows with gratitude.

Every single one who has touched my life, my words.
Thank you!

INTRODUCTION

Are you raising your child in a place far from your family? Are you concerned about the village your little one is missing out on? Do you worry about raising kind humans who make good choices?

Does the world we are raising our kids in frighten you? Do you constantly wonder if your child will grow up to respect their heritage? Worry that they will someday lose their way?

I see you. I am you.

But more importantly, I have been where your child is today.

Raised toggling between two worlds, I am now parenting children rooted in multiple cultures. The current cultural conversations that exist during their growing years are a huge source of concern. It is more important than ever today to stand strong in holding our children's hand guiding them through life.

The moment you cuddle your infant in your arms for the first time, you experience love you didn't know was possible. Something else you didn't know you had within you, is **fear**. Endless. Constant.

The kind that leaves you with butterflies in your stomach. The constant second guessing yourself as you make parenting decisions is exhausting and frankly, needless. It takes so much away from the joy of the now.

"Am I doing a good job as a parent?", is something we ask ourselves every moment. No two parents experience parenthood the same way, but every single parent goes through similar emotions at different times in this journey.

This book empowers you to counter the fears that come with parenting in a generation where judging another is much easier than looking inwards.

You cannot stop your little ones from growing up and walking into the big bad world, but you can create within them the strength to face it. Every challenge, every fear.

Develop a confident mindset for yourself and your child. Build a faith within, about how you have raised your child. So, when they go out in the world, you need not fear for their future for you have faith that they will make empowered choices.

The Secrets Lie Within Our Own Childhood

Subconsciously, we imbibe our childhood growing up. In every situation we either mimic our parents or do the complete opposite by learning from their mistakes. This is a simple truth we need to consciously be aware of.

In Kuwait, a land far from which we belonged, our one-bedroom apartment was our world. Family friends were uncles, aunts and substitutes for the family that creates the village in which a child is raised (In India). In an Arab country, Rajput Indians with Christian Indian/Arabi neighbors and South Indian friends all through life who spoke every language other than Hindi, my world was always multicultural.

My mom pampered me, scolded me, talked to me endlessly

about everything under the sun as I sat on the kitchen counter absorbing her love for me. An idyllic world of a happy child. When I was ten, Iraq invaded Kuwait. And our little haven was destroyed. Literally. We took refuge in our home country India during the Gulf war where life was so different than I was used to.

Who are you? a question most often asked, baffled my 10-year-old mind. I realized early that your identity matters to others. It also dawned on me that I was content in the versatility of my upbringing. Confusing as it was to those around me. *I was pretty much the "Girl from Nowhere" compared to others who knew exactly where they were from.* Yet, I was never disoriented about who I was. Secure in the knowledge that being a good person mattered far more.

When Life as a Mom Finally Came

Being alone through motherhood has been an eye opener. Your village is made up of you, your close circle of friends, school and wonderfully kind strangers even. Many days your child's village is just you.

Through all my parenting though, I always look intuitively towards my childhood. Introspecting over my own life experiences and reactions. In fact, my journey as a world citizen is extremely beneficial to my children, as their experiences are not singular in dimension.

My children just like me, belong everywhere.

Why You Need This Book

By observing parents and current trends, I realize there is an immense need for balanced parenting strategies. These days, there are various belief systems made up of whatever the current parenting guru says to follow. Ideologies take over what was essentially *just parents being parents, as humanly and lovingly as possible.* Mumbo jumbo that turn your own beliefs into an abstract thought. You fear being labeled.

Being a guardian is just about providing empowerment early to children, so they can navigate life.

After all, why would we choose to complicate one of the most meaningful things we are going to do in our lives? The legacy we leave behind.

Conversing with empathetic people who are ahead of the curve provides me with unique insight. Often parents forget their own challenges with passing time and begin to make light of others' parenting struggles. And thus, it is very important to learn from each other as we grow together as parents.

I have been writing about cultural challenges parents face for 7 years now. The work led me to writing for various parenting magazines, blogs and news outlets. Over time I became aware that my voice alone was not enough and founded the Raising World Children, online magazine which brings together parents, educators from around the world. *My research and best practices have given birth to this book.*

Here are simple strategies to build a strong mindset. It provides you with the framework within which the vine of your family can grow. I pass on the light of my experience, so you may not wander in darkness, scared. But own your light and shine it upon those who you love the most. Your children!

Strong Roots
For
Sound Beginnings

1. EMPOWER YOUR PARENTHOOD

Breathe.

No one is born a perfect parent, with perfect kids. To get kids to do anything takes a huge amount of patience and perseverance. As a parent, you must constantly work on building the foundation on which their lives grow.

Parenting is akin to building a sand castle on the edge of the ocean. What you do seems to constantly get washed away. The frustration is understandable. But trust me, you eventually end up creating a masterpiece that's strong enough to weather the worst storms.

Children are blank pieces of colored paper that we create timeless art on.

I say colored paper because your child already is someone. Think about it. Every pregnancy is different because every single child is different. And every child's personality is different because with experience, our parenting choices evolve.

My children are as dissimilar as chalk and cheese. I made many decisions differently when I learned from my experience with my son. Also, taking care of a baby while parenting another affects decision making.

As parents, we can only raise children to be mindful. What they choose to do after a point is a sum of all the experiences they have had and a mindset that we foster. As a society, we need to take responsibility for that.

Before you can embark on the journey of developing an empowered mindset for your child in an ever-changing world, you need to reinforce the structure within which your child will grow. Your "self."

Loving Your Kids Takes Work

Sure, your baby has the potential to be the best thing to happen to humanity but the first few nights you stay awake are enough to make you question your decision to become a parent. Your child will constantly retaliate, throw tantrums, fight your every decision.

Being human, our child's actions/words hurt us. You will cry, pick yourself up and get back to wondering every day if all this work is worth it.

Wanting what's right for them and working towards it incessantly is the job description. And still be gentle with your baby because it just doesn't know any better. Your persistence matters. And *that* holds truer as they grow.

Think about it. Brushing teeth is second nature to you now, but a toddler who doesn't even talk, does not know why it's important.

Observe and Adapt

As a mother, your biggest job is to find what works for your family.

2

A *lot* of parenting is paying attention to how your child is. No one can possibly know your child better than you. The person who spends the most time with a child will always be the one who knows what works best with them.

Notice the little things. You will have to constantly focus on what is unique about your child and how to use it to help them make better choices. A lot of things come naturally to them. A lot needs to be worked upon. Use what they are inclined towards to help them learn.

Whenever teaching your child a new life lesson, you must go through a series of trials and errors. And remember the following.

Parenthood is very subjective.

What works for someone else might not work for your child. Take advise from every person you meet, if you will but make sure to adapt it to your little one's personality. Be sure to not overwhelm anyone in the family while doing so, yourself included.

Trust Your Instincts

This ties into the above. Over the course of this book, we will go over many ways in which to empower your child through life's many challenges. When things go wrong, and they often will, remember you being a parent must stay calm. You have a duty to go through every aspect of a situation, get to the cause and take appropriate action. Through it all, always trust your judgement. You know more than you think you do.

If something feels wrong, it probably is. Whether with the environment your child is in, a person, a situation or your own child. Be aware of the blind spot you have for your child even. Never fear taking well thought through action.

Plan and Then Have a Back Up Plan

Research everything and have a plan of action. And if all goes south, have a backup plan. This is especially useful for training kids, travel and birthday parties. Everything needs to be mapped while being aware that nothing will go the way you envision it and that's okay too. Everything works out just the way it's meant to be. Have faith.

Let Go of Little Things

This is a lesson we need to imbibe. Letting go is a conscious decision you need to make constantly. Know when to take breaks, let the laundry be or leave shopping for another day. Whatever takes the pressure off you.

Messes are going to be a big part of your life here on. Take stock of it. Worry about something and plan for disasters before they happen. After, just focus on what needs to be done to work on a solution. Work with your child towards learning the lesson that comes with the situation. Of course, if the situation warrants, consequences should be handed out too. But in case of accidents, just take a deep breath.

If something does not affect life in the next 5-10 years, let go.

Decide Your Parenting Location with Confidence

Stay at home or go back to work. Is this something you are struggling with?

Working parents worry they are giving too less time to their kids and stay at home parents worry about not being a good enough role model for their child. Each fears the advantages the other kind of lifestyle could provide a child. Both fear the stress the other kind of life would bring to their own mental state.

I know the debate of stay at home vs working parents is ongoing and very sensitive. I've heard working mothers wonder what stay at home moms do all day with the kids. I've been with stay at home parents who wish they had those "easy" 8-9 hours away from the grind. But both know in their hearts that, at the end of the day there is really no end to the work of a parent.

A working parent does not clock out of parenthood. Stay at home parents don't sit at home drinking wine while the kids watch TV.

This decision just defines where you will be parenting from. Worrying, learning experiences and scheduling conflicts are something that will remain constant.

What is essentially common though is the desire to raise children to be self-reliant and empowered. This can happen only when you make sure to parent in all the time that you are with your child. And find child care that cares for your child as they would their own. With love and using every teachable moment.

No matter where you are parts of your day, you are from the second you find out to eternity, a parent first.

There is no question of being this or that kind of parent. These are just labels, that have no real meaning.

Many of us don't even have a choice. If you are lucky enough to have a choice, how do you come about this life altering decision?

It's simple, really. Think about what makes you happy.

Being a parent is about making your children happy and happiness is water in a cup. Unless you are overflowing with it, there is nothing you can give another. This may sound cliché but if you choose to stay at home but would rather be working, you will surely start to resent it and vice versa. The core of all anger and unhappiness comes from resentment of unfulfilled desire. And it only grows.

My husband and I always wanted me to stay at home with the kids in their formative years. Both our mothers while passionate about life in their own ways took the decision to be at home with us in our early years and that is a huge part of who we are. My decision was also because I wanted to be the person my kids came to with every boo boo, laugh, milestone and reason they feel upset. I wanted to be the first person to mold my kids. It was a calculated *choice*.

I never expected it to be so lonely, frustrating and challenging. It was especially difficult when my husband started travelling. It took a toll, being with the kids 24/7, using every teachable moment, being there all...the...time.

And then I started my freelancing business and the monumental work on the Raising World Children magazine. My work fuels my passion while I do my bit to build a better world for my kids. The phrase "working from home "became a challenge we took on as a family facing new struggles.

It took me a while to create the balance of motherhood and entrepreneurship. We evolved as a family and found ways to make it all work. There are certainly sacrifices and creativity involved in being a one income family running a business. I am always exhausted to the core. Yet, I am constantly content. All those frustrations came hand in hand with those memories we created.

The truth though is that not everyone can be happy sitting on a park bench, looking out at kids on a hot day. Or the solitude of working from a desk in your bedroom with weird working hours, early morning, late into the night after the kids sleep.

I have friends who thrive on their 9-5 job and the environment it provides It genuinely makes them happy. The financial security helps them feel relaxed enough to be a better parent.

No matter what you choose, make sure to do what makes You a better parent. You need to find that one thing that makes you feel complete. It is important for your children to see you flourishing as a person.

Motherhood will always be a big part of your life, but that's all it is. A part of your life.

As you decide this big decision of where you parent from, remember

- You do you. Think about what makes you truly happy.
- There is no competition between parents.
- Everyone has a right to their choices.
- Guilt has no place in your decision.
- Doing what's best for your child means making the hard decisions.
- The world will judge you no matter what you do. All your need to do is stop judging yourself.
- Your child will be inspired by you, no matter what you choose to do.

Being your child's hero is a monumental perk of parenting.

Be Present During Parenting

Children need an environment in which they feel comfortable exploring, being themselves. Remember, early life lessons create the base of their entire lives.

So be a parent when you are present.

In today's digital age, parents are in serious risk of phoning in their parenting time, literally. Scrolling on their phones or letting the kids be busy on their gadgets during the precious time they have together.

It requires a lot of mindful discipline on our part to be present in the moment. Even taking pictures and videos of children, often takes away from the miracle of the moment.

A great example of this is taking videos of your child's recital. Do you realize you saw the whole recital through a camera lens worrying if anyone was in front of the camera? But you have forgotten to exist in that precious time when the child was looking out at you. All they see is you with a camera in front of you. They don't see the pride or joy you feel. All my performances, I would always find my parents in the crowd, my dad winding his moustache with pride.

The amount of time you parent is no guarantee for the kind of parenting you do when you are with the child.

Don't Wait for Sick Days to Relax

Sick Day = Henceforth known as the only day when you give yourself permission to lie down and take rest. And even then, your heart sinks at the thought of all the dropped balls and all the mental tabs in your head light up to things you should ideally be doing.

Strong Roots Have No Fear

When I was young, I used to get very angry at my mother.

She would tinker around the house cooking, cleaning, clearing up the clutter, and irritated with everyone when it was crystal clear to anyone looking at her that she was in fact too sick to be doing any of it. An expat with no familial support, she wanted to do it all. I wish now I had done more around the house.

Cut to today. I have a home to maintain. Two kids. A husband. To care for and feed. Not to mention other commitments Adult responsibilities. And like caregivers everywhere, I've developed the innate need to keep going on and on.

Whether I'm in pain or sick or worse, I keep the house clutter free, the kids' routines maintained as best as I can, and work on all that needs to be done to keep all the plates up in the air.

It's mostly me. I need to be sick in a clean house. Somehow the cleanliness outside makes me feel better inside—like dressing up when I'm in a bad mood. I wish someone would be there to pick up the slack to help my husband. Knowing it's just us here, I do what I can despite his protests.

Readymade food and my mother are missed terribly on these days.

After all, it's hard for one person, especially the secondary caregiver, to suddenly keep track of the multitude of working parts in home life. When I'm sick, the clutter grows in every direction. The laundry piles up high. And each day off means a week of work—not to mention the catching up that needs to be done at work. The work-life tightrope that we so precariously walk daily gets loose and close to impossible to navigate.

My friends who are moms get it. They understand why, when they call to check on me, they find me busy cleaning or putting away the dishes. They encourage me to rest but empathize that it's hard for a mother to get those naps in, especially if the kids are young with the mess growing exponentially in your sleep-induced absence.

The fear of the loss of that fine balance makes us frenzied, and we get to work as soon as the fever subsides, or the painkillers take effect. This fear needs to be put to the side while we recuperate. We need to remember that we need to be at a 100% and need to put our time into what's needed to thrive.

I recently had someone comment to me on the fact that I had the *"luxury of girls night out"*. Another day, I felt a ton of guilt as I spent an hour talking on the phone with a friend when I should have been working on this very book instead. Girls night, phone conversations and me time are not luxuries or guilty pleasures. These are basic needs that one needs in order to prosper.

And most important is time you give to your "self" that feeds your soul.

The unicorn I'm referring to, is the time during which you, in solitude do something that truly excites you. In which you create something or learn something, get your hands dirty or get your inner fire going.

You can feel your mind, heart expanding. You feel victorious. The time when the reason for your smile is you, no one else. The quiet time in which you experience your soul growing.

How many of us do that?

And when we do get a few precious minutes we pick some random item off the ever-expanding list in our head and we use that time to get the so-called job done. This needs to stop.

I remember when my first kid was born, every mother told me," Sleep when the baby sleeps." And you know what? I just couldn't. I either stayed awake catching up on chores or planning stuff or spending time with family that would soon leave or funnily, I would just stay awake looking at my child. Romantic as the last reason was, I should have just slept!

A bitter truth is that people often revel in the knowledge that our family depends on us for everything. As much as we crib through each day, we specially love being there for the ones we love in every way possible.

The world can go on without us, if only we stop spinning for a while. We need to remember to love ourselves too.

It is not easy, but we have to fight for it just as much as anything else we love. As much as we need to let off steam and spend time with friends and roam around outside of home all by ourselves, we need time to enjoy being alone. To be there for the people we love, we need to stay healthy, strong, loving, patient and most of all happy. Simply because every person deserves it.

Even when we do live those precious, much needed selfish moments for ourselves, we are doing it for our loved ones. Happiness is a fickle emotion. The more we give, the more we get. But the more we expect others to contribute to it, the more disappointed we are bound to get.

Of the many things there are to do by yourself is -
- Take up a hobby that needs you to use your creativity and hands.
- Plan that girl's night out and laugh with your friends.
- Join a book club and enjoy productive cultural conversations.

- Get a massage.
- Practice self-love, maybe through reading or exercise.
- Take a class by yourself.
- Pick up a project that you do just because it makes you happy.

Change things up. Connect your inner being with things other than your family and chores. And don't ever feel guilt or fear for all that's there behind you. All of it will be right there when you get back, rejuvenated and relaxed.

The only thing between your" Me Time" and you are a dozen chores that need doing, yes. But mainly just You.

Seeing you live a wholesome life, being productive in your working hours and your down time even, is inspiring your child in every way.

Find Your Tribe

Parenting is lonely. No one talks about how singular life within a family unit gets. A parent needs a lot to keep the vigor alive. Chief among them is the right tribe.

You need to find your people. This too takes work and time. It is so important to have a non-judgmental group holding you up. Yes, your partner is there but you are going to need an extended group of people around you who support you, your choices, your dreams - no matter what.

People in different stages of life, who are your cheerleaders. Those who wish you well, in spite your successes. Those who show you the right path when you are failing. Those who laugh with you when your child does that funny thing. Those who can relate with you when your child exasperates you. Those who tell you that this is all nothing compared to what their older child is putting them through now. Those who challenge your thought process, even.

Above all, be someone's tribe too. Don't wait for kind gestures. Be the first one to reach out with a hand in friendship.

Recognize and Keep Negativity at Bay

People will have opinions on your life. There's a huge difference between voicing your opinion and judging someone's choices. Understand it, accept the first with grace and let go of the latter. You cannot control the way someone opinionates.

The only person who you can control is you.

Another thing to be wary of is drama - family, friendship, life or at work. The kind where you end up talking about something incessantly, contributing to the complexity by giving your voice to it. You need not. Talking about something relentlessly, with different people helps no one. Any conversation you have should be productive and adding to the life you share with those around you.

Find a solution or act. Do not become a part of the problem.

Negative energies will drain away your positive vibes. As will negative people. Take stock of this math of life. Be mindful of what is not serving you and subtract it by walking away.

Your children need to know about the world. But they do not need to know why someone is being horrible to you or why the in laws are being unfair. Kids are super perceptive, anyway. You do not need to spell everything out for them.

Keep your personal fights and frustrations to yourself. It turns to bitterness and angst within them. And that is something no child needs early in their lives.

Weigh Your Words

Being a parent means constantly being proven wrong. When you tell someone, your child doesn't eat something, they will. The minute you say to someone your child never does something, they will. So before stereotyping your child's actions, be wary of what you say.

Children hear everything, even when they aren't paying attention. So be kind with your words. To them. About others.

Even when you reprimand them, make sure to keep sarcasm and swear words away.

Children mimic people around them. That thing you say to them in the heat of the moment. Trust me. It will come back to you.

Do NOT Compare

Our minds know it, but when we see another kid doing something ours isn't, we tend to worry about our child. Don't. Every child hits their milestones, physical and mental at different times in their lives.

We stress, wondering if we are doing everything to help our child thrive. But when we talk about how so and so is doing this or try to use competition to push our child ahead, we are essentially saying, "You are not enough."

That doesn't mean you stop trying to push them, but 'Comparisonville' is a bad place to live in.

Your child is enough. So are you!

Remember to Laugh

The best way to get through any struggle is with humor. When you can find the humor in any situation, you win. In a few days, what seemed like life or death will become a hilarious anecdote. Like all those surprising ways your child creates messes.

And what you cannot make jest of, breathe through. It will pass!

They are going only little once. Enjoy those milestones.

There is so much pressure on kids today to do every possible activity under the sun. To make them independent early. Educate them. Keeping them busy every minute of every day, is a humongous undertaking. For them.

Let them enjoy their childhood. Enjoy it with them. Breathe in every moment.

They have many years ahead of them to be part of the rat race that is life. They are only little once. You both have only this time together now. Before you know it, they will be out of the house. Take those walks with them, take in every memory they provide.

The best lessons are learned in the simplest of life's messy, unplanned moments.

Parenthood is an endless roller coaster. Even if you are overwhelmed, don't ever close your eyes. Your child needs you and your love every minute. This ride isn't going to last forever.

Raising children takes tenacity, ferocious will and fighting every day when all you desire is to just let go and sleep. Tears threaten when you are feeling helpless in teaching them essential life skills. The guilt is tremendous, and yet, we know, if we give up on an important thing that needs to be taught, our child will eventually suffer.

Yielding to a child's will is easy. Standing tall as an example 24/7 for love, for values, to show your child the right way, that is what makes a parent amazing!

2. CHANNEL BIG EMOTIONS

Skating. Swimming. Cycling. And any time my mother would apply gram flour to my face, I would raise hell!

Yelling, crying like there was no tomorrow. A 3-10-year-old fearing for my life. Scared I would get hurt. Hating that yellow paste on my face with vengeance. Wondering why in the world is she putting me through torture!

That and performing in front of a crowd.

She in her pride would want to show off her daughter's dancing prowess. And said daughter would cry and cry because ... honestly, even I don't know why I cried. I was a stage performer from the age 4 for goodness sake!

What I do know is, I was a kid not understanding why in the world would we need any of these life skills?! I was against a huge mountain (my mom), unrelenting. I wailed, trying to get my way but, in my heart, I always knew she would not deter till I walked her path. Still, I never stopped trying to get away with it.

The insistent crying, the yelling. The muttering of horrid things with no real thought and then half an hour later regretting everything. An hour later promising myself I would never do it to only do it all over again the next time. My brain a fog of my stubbornness.

Do you remember yourself as a child? We all have done it in a given phase of our lives. That's what allows our mothers to proudly, and happily defend their grandchildren when we complain about them. "You were no different!", they gleefully say.

And yet, we expect our children to be the epitome of perfection in behavior.

When I Became a Mom

When my child fights with me, in the heat of the moment, I get this huge lump in my throat. My cheeks get hot and I pray to somehow get through to my child on whatever it is I need them to do. "It's all my chickens coming home to roost", I moan to myself. And when the moment passes, this one simple thought warms my heart,

"In spite of all the times my moms pushed me outside my comfort zone, I knew I was loved. My mom never once gave up and that is why I learned."

I knew my parents would never stop trying. Even today, they often push me to make better choices.

The Place of Emotions in Your Child's Life

- Venting in a place they consider safe.
- Building a bond with you.
- Expressing what they cannot verbalize
- Learning to process bad experiences.
- Empathizing with others when they feel the same.
- Testing boundaries to push for what they want.

When Big Emotions are Labeled as Sensitivity

"He's too sensitive. It will be hard for him, being sensitive in this world.", a concerned relative remarked. My son would cry when saying goodbye. In a time when meeting people was limited to playdates and preschool, he and his sister would bawl when saying goodbye.

This sadness in the face of separation (a natural and beautiful proof of caring) was seen with disappointment. It is unfortunate when today, instead of empowering our children, we choose to label their feelings as weakness. Rather than finding the source of their discomfort or teaching them to better handle those big feelings (we all feel even as adults), we sweep it under the useless, hurtful carpet of "being too sensitive" or "too stubborn" or as "a phase they need to grow out of."

No Kid is Tantrum Free

The first time your child does it, you will wish the earth swallows you whole! Your ears will burn, and you will feel like everyone is judging you for being the worst parent with the "brat raising hell on the floor." Trust me. You are not going to be the first or last mother on earth with a child like that.

Relax! Most moms are just nodding their heads in understanding, feeling bad for your bad day or getting teary eyed about when their little ones were that young and easier to handle.

Every person at every age, throws tantrums. Why do we expect little ones with no awareness of their surroundings to know better?

How you deal with people at their worst is what defines your relationships.

- Don't make the tantrum your focal point.
- Don't worry about the world around you.
- Do Not give in to any non-essential demand.
- Don't forget to talk about what happened after.
- Take a moment to try to empathize with them.
- Make a point to acknowledge their emotion while redirecting them towards healthier expression.

And this is true of every relationship.

When my son was a toddler, I overheard a girl scolding her little brother. She said, "Look at me. Listen to my words. You must (enter corrected behavior here). And then she made him repeat it back.

It was astounding that this little girl knew what we need to do to make sure kids comprehend what we are conveying. I learned with time that this is a useful process because children having misbehaved always dart their eyes away from the person who is reprimanding them. To hide like the cat with closed eyes drinking milk imagining no one else can see it.

People are born defiant, expressive, emotional, curious and stubborn. They want what they want when they want it.

It is no surprise then that children will cry, stomp and wail to get their way. They will push boundaries to see how far they can push your buttons. Meanwhile, you question your every move as a parent, wondering what course to take in caring for another person's emotional needs.

A parent recently lamented to their child, "Why are you being so stubborn?", I responded. "He's two. He's being a child. Now repeat your sentence saying, "Why are you being a child?" See how silly it sounds?

Sadness. Loneliness. Desire. Greed. Envy. And more. We need

to remember that everyone gets overwhelmed when they feel big emotions. So, children need to be given that space in which to express.

Adults are nothing but children in bigger bodies. What we learn to do with time is better hide our first reaction and give out a processed one.

Validating emotions requires –

- Identifying emotions through introspection.
- Processing emotions skillfully.
- Responding appropriately.

How do we teach kids when we ourselves are adapting?

Look for the Cause

It is important to remember; every single child expresses instantly what they feel. And when they do internalize, it is because they feel their expression will not be accepted.

As parents we need to look for the cause of an outburst or reaction. Is it that the child is lacking sleep, energy, food or maybe it is some deficiency that is making them bad listeners or lazy even.

Observe their patterns. Write it down, if needed.

Give Them Time to Process

Take the time to wait for those feelings to fade. If it's a pointless tantrum, do not react. Tell them you will wait for them to calm down. Or engulf them in a hug. Or maybe for your child, it might be best to just remove yourself from the equation all together.

There are times when my child just gets worse with me being there, so I accept someone else's help. When they have calmed down even a bit, first thing is to give them a hug or the solution or calmly ask what exactly it was that they felt or needed.

Be a Good Listener

It is so important for kids to know that their voice is heard. That they can comfortably talk about what they are feeling without judgement. As parents, we tend to instantly react to an emotion instead of waiting for the disruptive behavior to fade and then use our listening ears.

Listening is important if you are to be an advocate on your child's behalf.

Be Persistent with the Solution Needed

Life gets busy. We get weighed down. Regardless, we have to be consistent in our efforts to be proactive in countering the cause of our child's triggers. Like, if more sleep is their need, then a standard bedtime must be worked on, as many trials and errors it needs to help them get to that point.

If what they need is more people time, plan extra playdates. Plan out time and work hard towards it. No, do not feel guilty if you cannot do it all the time. Yes, try your best to work towards the goal.

Trial and error. Consistently.

Encourage Emotional Independence

When kids are secure in the knowledge that they have enough, they want for nothing. This applies to emotional independence as well. All kids really want is us, our time. It helps them be more emotionally independent.

Since they know the one place where they can express is available to them whenever needed. When I work, my kids know I cannot be disturbed but they have the freedom to play beside me. For you, it might be just snuggle time before bed.

It is wonderful. This strength that is born of those precious moments of just being.

Be a Good Emotional Example

When you accept your emotions and work towards a better response, kids learn to do the same. Being human, we tend to often explode in our response to hurt. Take the time to accept your folly/choice of expression and explain to the kids. Your child may tease you later (they all do!) but they will think twice themselves before mimicking your wrong behavior too.

Parents need to set an example of owning up to mistakes.

Effective Communication

This is such a big part of being a child and learning. Give your child time to process their feelings and ask them later about what it was that affected them or what they had done wrong. Talk to them about -

- What they were thinking.
- Why their actions had an impact.
- How they process those big feelings.

Pretend Play Situations

This is a fun exercise to do when kids are in a happy mood. "What would you do if …". I give them outrageous responses as answers myself and kids being kids, love telling parents what they are doing wrong and how to handle something better. A great way to foster logical thinking.

Do not Solve Their Problems

Don't jump in to solve their problems. Let them have the time to figure out a solution. Give them a hug. A little time to let them feel what they are feeling and use logical thinking is wonderful for growth. After all, you will not be able to go to their school to help them when they face unique challenges with friends and society.

Promote an Attitude of Gratitude Early

A big reason of emotional issues and discontent is harboring resentment. Promote early the knowledge that being grateful makes us content with what we have and thus happier.

Adults tend to focus on what's gone bad in their day. As do children. A way to counter this is when I started doing the following with my kids. We discuss one good thing, one bad thing and what we did to turn a bad situation into a good one.

Looking at every problem as an opportunity is a wonderful trait to develop.

Also, focus constantly in passing conversation about what we have that we need to be grateful for. Specially, bringing thought to how everyone has different advantages in life. This is especially important to incorporate during meal conversations, festive seasons and birthdays.

Forgive One Offs

You know your child. If they are behaving erratically after a long day or when they are hungry, and it is not in their nature to be that way, forgive their responses.

This applies to you as well.

You have only so much patience in your bucket and children have a way of draining it. It gets very hard after the 15th time you have requested them to eat or pick up their toys or put away their shoes, especially if you are getting late for something but hang in there. When your frustration or exhaustion blows up, forgive yourself those blow ups. But as far as possible, when you feel the overwhelm, step away and come back rebooted, fresh.

Patience too takes practice.

Don't let emotions become bigger than you. Take the time to self-analyze yourself as well as your child. When you look at your situation from the outside, the big bad problems seem much smaller.

3. DISCIPLINE THROUGH KARMA

Years ago, a mother once lamented while her two-year-old son climbed carelessly high over the TV cabinet, "I cannot help it. He is so naughty. How much can I scold him? I don't want him hating me for being a stern mom."

I didn't have kids then, but the thought left me surprised. I have been scolded and nagged a lot. I have never *hated* my mom. I still stand by what I said then,

"No child would hate their parent who rightly, and consistently does course correction. They eventually are always grateful for the guidance."

An oft repeated Indian tale comes to mind. A mother adored her son. So much so that she never scolded him. Never stopped him from doing anything wrong. Even covered for him. Over time, he went from being spoilt to lying to stealing and before long he was in jail. When his mother came to visit him, he called her close and yelled at her, "Why didn't you yell at me that first time I was being rude to you?"

After all, life's every moment is made up of two paths. Each decision leading you to a different course, creating this labyrinth that is life. When I look at all that I'm grateful for today, I can trace it all back to a decision based on a mindset honed over time.

Watchful Eyes

My brother and I would often catch my mom staring at us. We would be playing, dancing, walking or even eating and she would be gazing at us. Now this was never a lost in thought look. It was always a freaky 'I'm looking at everything you do' look.

At any social event I always knew she was watching. She knew what I was doing. This look that made me prickle all over, feeling like I'm the only one in the room and I need to do what I'm doing right! If I was behaving badly, I would turn around and sure enough her eyes would grow stern and I changed my track.

It felt intrusive. It irritated my brother and myself. We would snap at her to "cut it out," or "Stop staring," or we just stopped what we were doing.

Till one day, after becoming a parent, I realized that I too watch my children … constantly! I love everything they do. It is almost like a guilty pleasure. At social events, if I can't see them, my ears are listening for their sounds. Everything they do is special because for me, these people that I created are doing many of those things for the very first time.

I fly back to all those moments when mom stared. It wasn't sternness she felt or perfection she desired. It was just her love. *Her desire to see us.*

It is that love that kept me from doing wrong. Always nudging me towards the right path. It played a huge part in making me mindful, introspective and eventually affected a lot of life altering decisions.

Reprimand when I· misbehaved. Lectures when I did not

follow instructions. Stern looks from across the room, when I was being naughty. And even the rare smack when I was being extremely disrespectful. After all, slapping kids was a big part of Indian parenting two generations ago when time outs were not as popular through American shows. And always the constant reminders about what the right behavior and choices look like, feel like.

None of it ever affected the love I had for my parents. For I always knew no one in the whole wide world loved me more than them.

Over time, I came to expect my mom's scolding. Not that I enjoyed them, but I was a child, testing boundaries. The time she caught me reading a comic when I should have been studying. When I painted on the walls, badly at that! When I took too long for homework or didn't eat my food. I didn't get away with any of it.

And today, I'm grateful for not being able to.

Understanding Karma's Role in Our Lives

At the playground, I saw a smaller boy saying something extremely offensive to an older one. The older boy, not to be disrespected started yelling at the boy to never say such things to anyone. Some spittle might have flown as the older one towered over him.

The younger boy ran to his father and complained that the older boy spit on him on purpose. The father oblivious to his own son's part in the argument, came over huffing and puffing, ready to take the older kid to task. The father had clearly assumed the fact that the two boys were from different cultures had a lot to do with it. Luckily, I was there to explain to him what his own son had done. And that the older boy while responding to disrespect had clearly not meant to intentionally spit.

The father calmed down but didn't admonish his son. Instead, he comforted him, saying, "Don't worry son. Karma will get him".

I couldn't believe my ears. The concept of Karma so blatantly misused! And then I realized how important it was for to explain to our kids how karma works in our lives.

Over the summer, I had seen this father dote on his child with things and misplaced love whenever he complained against a child. Never once wondering why his child alone was having issues with *every* child. I could predict the child's misdeeds would only grow.

For no child who does wrong can be held responsible. It is parents who stand by doing nothing, who are at fault.

It dawned on me early, the importance of parents in understanding how their actions affect their children and their mindset.

The Beauty of the Concept of Karma

The law of Karma is one which teaches us that all our thoughts, words and actions begin a chain of cause and effect, and that we will personally experience the effects of everything we cause. Much like the Butterfly effect.

We may not experience the consequences (the returning karma) right away, but just like dominoes falling one after the other we can usually trace back most things to our own doing.

People talk about having 'good karma' and 'bad karma'. I think actions are just actions, what is important is to accept our role in any given bad decision that came about. Very often, all the right things in our life are just miraculous opportunities which we say yes to. We need though to be able to recognize them as well. Just as we need to ensure our children derive the consequences of a bad decision when they see one.

Of course, fate has a big part in life too. That is what teaches us to let go when things are out of hand.

Until we understand our role in our child's behavior, we cannot really look upon them as culprits. We all hold power within us. The power within children needs to be unlocked by parents.

Disciplining My Children

Since, I was little my mom used say, "Aisi jagah baith mat, koi bole uth. Aisi baat bol mat, koi bole jhoot." That translates to - Never sit somewhere that causes someone to say move and don't say something that gives others an opportunity to call you a liar. The move part just means no other person should be able to point out your actions as wrong. Carry yourself with grace, dignity and poise.

And honestly, while I'm totally okay with it my kids being reprimanded if they deserve it, I would rather it need not happen. So, no wrong action is ignored, no needless pampering is done and no excuse for disrespect is entertained. I have constantly disciplined them since they were little, making sure they know they are loved. No matter what is going on with me or how tiring it is.

Spills made were cleaned by the kids since the age of 2. Once broken or lost, toys have not been bought again. A "no" has always been a firm no and I have always re iterated the difference between good and bad decisions. Explaining to them that often what happens wrong is a direct consequence of a wrong choice they have made.

This does not mean my children are saints. They still rebel. They still throw tantrums. They still feel the need to push their boundaries whenever they can.

But often enough I'm filled with joy when they are given compliments on being raised well or when they exhibit good decision-making skill. Like, when all his friends were kicking a small, newly planted tree down at school, but he chose not to. Or when he would rather play alone than play a game that seems wrong. When he chose to donate $1 for animal welfare instead of buying something for himself. When my daughter chooses to not stand by when a friend is getting pushed by another. Both kids have always shared their toys. Rarely climb on furniture. Respect their own toys as well as those of others'. Are kind to everyone and know when someone needs help.

Kids making sound decisions when not around parents is what matters. And that comes from us being with them even when we are not.

Be Strong in Your Nos Early

When you see them doing something they shouldn't be, stop them with a sharp No. They should learn early boundaries and how to respect them. How to respect toys and things that aren't theirs. Be consistent with your "Nos" and stern when you see misbehavior.

As they grow, the Nos become harder to stick to. You say no. A child asks again. You repeat your reason, they ask again. And if you are unlucky on an off day, you experience a tantrum. But stay strong. When parents say no first, and then give in children get mixed signals and never, ever get the lesson.

Be Instant in Your Reprimand

It often happens that you end up in a public scenario where you feel that it is okay to let the rules go. Overall, yes, you need to pick your battles, but a child needs to know immediately when something they do is extremely wrong. If you bring up that topic later, it really doesn't have the desired effect.

Be Assertive in Your Decisions

Children are great at figuring out who to manipulate and how. It is human to want to. If you waver, the confused child will constantly push boundaries. They will do this nonetheless, as part of growing up. But knowing that their parents stand their ground and are united, reduces push back.

In our home, a yes can become a no, but a no cannot become a yes.

As in, if dad says yes and mom says no, it's a no and if either says no, it is surely no. This gives our children the opportunity to put their argument or request forward knowing what the possible outcomes are. They never try to divide and conquer and know their parents have a united front and one of the two can possibly be wrong in decision making and the other will course correct as needed.

Try Out Different Consequences

When it was time for her medicine, my almost 2-yr-old daughter closed her mouth, turned around and said, "I want timeout instead."

While it is important for kids to have consequences, you cannot really be sure what works to sink in the lesson for your child in what situation. Every moment in a child's life is unique. You need to figure out what works best. Sometimes timeouts work, other days taking game time away. Other times you may get a better result from giving an incentive in place for them. Keep trying.

A good consequence is effective but not overwhelming. I personally am not in favor of incentives that are toy, monetary or candy based. Be creative in what consequences would work. Again, knowing your child is a big part of this.

Be Careful with Your Words

Make sure you do not give a negative connotation to their character vs their behavior which can possibly have a lasting impact. Eg, saying, "This was you doing something wrong." Not, "You are a bad boy.". No matter how angry you are, keep the venom of sarcasm and doubt from your words away. Remember they are much younger than you. Be a parent, not a bully.

Your Time Together Counts

This may seem obvious but a healthy relationship with your child is a necessary foundation for discipline. Often children act out just to get attention. If your child is being very disruptive, introspect if insecurity might be a reason. If your child loves and respects you, consequences will be much more effective. Make the most use of time spent with them.

Explain the Role of Karma in Consequences

Coming back to Karma, it is a wonderful concept to share with your child. Tell them how every action has an equal and opposite reaction. Science! If they are careless with their toy, it will break. When they create spills, they ought to clean it up. Disrespect will get reprimands. This helps a child slowly learn to first take ownership of their actions and the predictive nature of their actions.

Consequences should be used as a teaching tool and shouldn't shame or embarrass kids. In fact, those type of punishments make behavior problems worse, not better. And remember, if you are constantly handing out timeouts and reprimands, kids are sure to become desensitized.

If you can't think of a logical consequence, ask the misbehaving child for the next time. Kids are great at thinking up consequences. That way they learn to take ownership of their actions.

Pick Your Battles

Raising kids is a game of awareness of energies. It takes a lot out of you to do the work that is needed. Be conscious about where you spend your limited amount of enthusiasm.

Every fight is not worth fighting. This applies to every relationship, specially your own child.

You don't want to waste time on arguments that do not carry a life altering consequence. Does it really matter what your child wears to preschool? No. Does it matter if your child wears a jacket in subzero temperatures. Yes. You get the idea.

Give Kids Limited Options

Often the simplest solution to avoiding battles of wills is making kids aware in advance of their options. So, every time my son needs to wear appropriate clothes to an occasion, I give him options the night before. When children know what to expect, often they are mentally prepared of what comes next and are better equipped to act accordinly.

Use Every Teachable Moment

Try to be proactive in teaching kids about how to behave given any situation. When you see another child behaving badly at the store or in a show talk to your child about better behavior given the same situation. Putting a child's bad behavior into positive perspective is a great opportunity for you to help the child learn something.

Sometimes the children are just genuinely ignorant about the "badness" inherent in their actions. All kids need is a strong but loving conversation about why you don't want them doing what they're doing.

4. IMBIBE MULTILINGUISM

All my life, I have asked for translations.

First from my mom to translate what she was speaking to her family (Marathi). Not to mention being surrounded by people who spoke Arabic, a language I can read but not understand. Then friends at college (Malayalam, Tamil) and at work (Arabic, Konkani etc). Once, I got married, I needed my husband to translate what he spoke to his friends (Gujarati).

It felt endless. And I wondered why people couldn't be more empathetic to those who didn't know a language. I wished my mom had persisted in teaching me Marathi, her mother tongue so I too would have a clique with at least Maharashtrians around the world. After all, most Indians are trilingual or more. Many speak English, some Hindi and are fluent in one or more other language.

Unfortunately, when my mother tried teaching me, I apparently confused English, Hindi with Marathi turning it into an alien code and our existence in a Hindi speaking household negated the need to learn more than two languages.

With most people needing to box you into a language category so that they can instantly build a rapport, I was at a constant disadvantage. Language became more a divider than unifier. Others like me, who have been raised in a multicultural environment will understand the difficulties of being by yourself, category-less in life.

The feeling of being out of place came with many character perks though. I develop an instant respect for people who courteously speak in a common language when in a group. I appreciate when I don't have to ask, and a translation is provided generously. It gave me a better radar for people with an open, global mindset. Plus, I got bold in asking for translations as well.

Instead of cribbing about how people are alienating me, now I just ask them what they are talking about. Most people are grateful for the reminder since talking to their peers in their common language is just a lizard brain switch that happens naturally. Those who are not, bare not the courtesy of a second conversation anyway. Human instinct is hard to fight. Over the years, I also picked up quite a lot of Punjabi, Gujarati, Marathi, a bit of Tamil, Spanish and currently, my kids and I are learning American Sign Language.

Today my children reap the benefits, knowing early the importance of being open to language learning.

Our Struggle with Bilingualism

I am Indian. Ideally, Hindi would be my native language. The realization that English was my first language came to light one sunny, winter evening a few years ago. At the park, an elderly Indian lady approached my kids. Making small talk, she asked the standard questions about where in India did I belong, where I worked etc. After a few minutes of watching my son, she questioned, "Your son doesn't speak Hindi?"

When I replied that he understood but didn't speak, she retorted," But you stay at home, right?" How is it he hasn't learned? "I was livid! It was hurtful and insensitive on so many levels, my mind hurt.

A few days later though, it made me introspect. I wondered about the kids I knew who did speak their native language. Comparing all the things parents with native language speaking kids did differently than us, I asked questions. The most important answer that came across was," Speak to them only in that language." Easier said than done! That is when I observed that my husband and I speak in English to each other.

For the longest time, I never understood the basic reason of why my son, whose parents are both Indian didn't just naturally pick up the language?! Most of the kids I know who speak their native language have grandparents living with them for long periods of time. And slowly I realized out biggest folly! Parents who speak the language at home continuously have a better chance. At our home, my husband and I speak English more often than Hindi. When I started thinking about why, that is when I realized English is my first language and it is hard for me to remind myself constantly to talk in Hindi.

My son didn't speak but he understood Hindi completely, since the age of 2. We know because he retaliated whenever we happened to talk in Hindi about doing something he doesn't like. (Ha!) But when it comes to conversing, it was hard looking at the kids flounder for the right words to use. Also, time consuming. In the hurry to get on with our day, we often gave in and told them in English what we were saying in Hindi. We wouldn't stick with it.

Initially, my son would just say no to speaking only Hindi. In his head he was only American and since none of his friends in preschool or teachers spoke Hindi, he just didn't feel the need. It has been a couple of years of trial and errors and I am still working on the same. While, the barrier to learning Hindi has broken, our language learning is still in progress, specially since we are learning multiple at the same time.

Raising Multilingual Kids

I share my personal struggles to express how difficult it is for children to sometimes naturally grow to love and learn their mother tongue and how many people may find learning a new language hard or look at it as a barrier, especially if they feel left out.

There are though, many advantages to being multilingual for children -.

1. Connecting with grandparents and family back home.
2. People who are multilingual can be incredibly useful, particularly in certain fields where the ability to read or understand an original document can help lend additional information. This can open a world of opportunities.
3. The more languages you speak, the more people you can connect with.
4. If you enjoy traveling abroad, multilingualism will benefit you.
5. Developing empathy for others, as they too struggle to learn a new language.
6. Learning about cultures. When you use different techniques you naturally end up teaching your child about world cultures or even about subcultures from your own country.
7. Critical thinking and problem solving.
8. Patience is a key in learning about a new language.
9. Learn further languages more easily as they identify similarities in sound and script.
10. To help others when need be in understanding their own

culture.

Tips to Raising Multilingual Children

The best way is to speak to them in their native language from birth. Many parents worry that children will not learn English and be at a disadvantage at school, but children are resilient and can pick up languages fast. So, start early.

And even if you miss the boat as I did, take heart that there is no real age for learning languages. With persistence and below steps you can imbibe new languages at any age.

Be Consistent at Home

Have one parent talk in only one language at home. It can often get hard to see your child struggle with a new language. You must barrel through it. Kids usually understand a new language way before they start speaking it. Take advantage of that. Do requests in the new language. Repeat that in English if need be. Slowly they catch on.

Make Your Own Flash Cards

Draw simple things and teach your kids to say those very words every few days. Add three new words every day. One sentence. Revise what you have learned. Once kids start reading, stick them around the house if need be.

Story Telling is a Wonderful Resource

Consciously looking for books that were simple in diverse languages was a game changer for me. It is more palatable for kids to understand nuances when they can read word by word.

Search for books in the language. Get books from the library or borrow books from friends. Find resources online from reviews given. Reading cultural stories will also help teach children about the world they are trying to understand.

I had to make up simple stories since initially it was hard to find easily readable stories in new languages. As I made them up, slowly they started to as well. A fun activity.

Use Reminders

Post-Its, alarms on the phone, motivational quotes, pictures to remind your children and yourself to speak in the language you are working on. Attach it to something that you would do anyway. Like in our home, after bath, we would learn Hindi and sign language. Slowly the kids got used to practicing at that time, expecting it.

Use Rhymes and Prayers

Teach your kids rhymes or prayers in the new language. Two-line rhymes are easiest to remember. These help kids memorize. There are many videos online for the same.

Arrange Playdates

Try to organize playdates with kids who already speak the language. Children are naturally inclined to conversing with friends in a common language. Ask them for assistance.

Travel with Heart

For us, every trip to India or every visit around the world with family encourages language learning. Meeting people who are culturally similar makes for an associative desire to learn.

Create Games

There are many games online that help encourage the love of learning. Puzzles, drawings are fun ways to teach kids to identify words, form sentences etc.

Consume Content in Said Language

Watching movies and kids shows are a great way to explore a new cultures' linguistic perspective. This may seem like a very natural way to educate yourself, but it takes effort to find content appropriate for kids in any given language.

Acknowledge Their Efforts

I find my little ones talking in a new language when they want something. If it is within reason, we acquiesce to their request. They feel a pride in making that extra effort consciously for something they desire.

Understand that learning a new language doesn't come easily to every child. Some children are inclined to multilingualism. Others need to work harder. I have heard stories where children couldn't speak or were confused in multiple languages for a while before they caught on. *As was I.* This is not to say that EVERY child will have issues. It is just a process and it's harder for some than others.

Invariably though, with a little bit of consistent effort every one can be fluent in more than one language.

5. CREATE A LOVE OF READING

Every book is a world within itself.

Books are a very big part of my life. I started reading voraciously with Amar Chitra Katha and Archies; comics diametrically opposite in their cultures. Growing up, whenever I was on my own, books kept me company. They taught me about people and life, helping me grow. I never felt lost with a book in my hand. A solution to every problem just a read away.

Almost all creation begins with the written word. Unlock the imagination. Empower by igniting curiosity through reading.

Books are perhaps the biggest tool in your arsenal in teaching your kids about life skills, relationships, and the world. Words seeded deep in the soil of their mind. They have the power to grow inside — changing everything.

Every book does have magical powers. They create a relationship that stays with you and yours long after it leaves you. You can never forget a book that has transformed your life with a new perspective.

One of my favorite things about living in America is the free libraries. Book stores and libraries are my Disneyland. I go, I browse, and I come home with a bag full of treats to devour over a month's time. And now having access any title I want on my Kindle/iPad is just exhilarating, though nothing can ever replace the comfort of smells in old books and the rustling of turning pages.

Where books are concerned, I will always be a greedy little girl willing to pick up any comic, book, or magazine to discover the words that will forever transform me. Whenever I'm in a conundrum, I always trust there is someone out there feeling the same thing I am feeling and writing about it. And if I am lucky, I will find that book and read it.

Trips to the library are cherished in my household. As a parent, I am happy my kids love reading too. The turning of pages, the words coming alive, the curiosity aroused, the answers they find, are fascinating. There are many adventures one takes by losing ourselves in those rustling pages. More importantly, they help children broaden their horizons and create awareness.

As parents we can help children find all this and more by nudging them in the direction of the written word. The passport that gives an all access pass to new worlds.

Teaching My Kids the Importance of Reading

My son came back from pre-school all excited. The teacher had discussed the topic of Needs Vs Wants. He felt like such a big boy having grasped this essential aspect of life. We had fun discussing the various things we come across (toys are wants, food needs) until we came upon the topic of "Books". I said they are needs and he was sure that they are wants.

A few days later at a party, family friends and I started debating over the same. About how books are essential for a society and thus ideally should be a need. The children overheard this exchange and came over.

" Aunty, why do you say that books are a need?" a child asked.

Not one to leave a teaching moment, I asked the children, "What do you want to be when you grow up?"

"Doctor! Engineer! Astronaut! Policeman!" They shouted excitedly, hands reaching up high for their desired aspiration.

" How will you learn how to become one?"

" From a teacher," one responded.

" And your teacher will teach you by reading from a book someone has written about how to become an astronaut or engineer or doctor right?"

They all nodded.

" When you grow up and live by yourself you will want to cook or fix something. That time you will you look for a recipe in a book or read a manual right?"

Their heads kept moving in agreement.

"In old, old, old times when man discovered fire and hunting, they started scribbling on walls to teach others. So that no one ever forgot how to do them. First, they wrote on walls, then stone slabs, then long pieces of paper, then short pieces of paper that became books.

People need books to find out how to do things and teach others. And not just teaching; when people tell stories, we learn about what we should do or should not do in life. So maybe not all but some books are definitely a need, right?"

Their mouths forms "Ooohs!" while their tiny heads nodded

understanding. I could see a light go on in all their eyes!

Books are a gateway into the world of learning. More importantly, the core of all learning has reading at its core. There's a book for every problem. Even online, one must be able to scour through pages and pages of content before you find a solution.

People need books to find out how to do things and teach others. And not just teaching, when people tell stories, we learn about what we should do or should not do in the same situation.

How do you foster this life-long love of books?

Have a Fixed Time

Snuggling with kids and reading to them, has two-fold advantages. Education and Security. The distractions around you falling away as it's just you and your child exploring new worlds.

As with everything in life, something must be part of our daily routine in order to become a habit. Have a set time or day. Like bed time or holidays or weekends when they know there will be reading and make it an event into itself.

Let Them Pretend

After I read to her, my daughter would often say, "Now my turn" and make up a story along the lines of what we just read. Before I knew it she could recognize a few letters/words. My son always loved nonfiction more, so he enjoyed looking at pictures of dinosaurs, and the world. Pretending to be a part of history.

Help Them Read

Pause when you come across a word you are sure they know of. Just like cycling, let them read slowly and steadily till they start doing it on their own.

Write Their Name on The Books

Whenever they attain a book, write their name on the first page. From whom or the occasion. It helps them take ownership of the same. Also, it turns the book into a keepsake to be cherished.

Have Reading Parties

Kids love doing things as a group and showing off their stuff. Call a few friends over. Have them bring their favorite books. Read to them or if they are old enough, have them each read their most liked story. And then ask them questions about the book. Discuss what each one loves about it.

Books Make Great Gifts/Goody Bags

You have lot of options at your local discount stores or dollar stores to give as goody bags. If you know the child, give them something that is to their liking. If not, you can choose something to the theme of the party or something age appropriate. Add fancy wrapping paper, their name and a candy if you like.

Give Kids Ample Choice

Let your children choose the books they would like to read. For the longest time it was a struggle for me to get my son to read stories but one day I realized his heart lay in reading nonfiction. Books about facts! And he hasn't stopped since. Let kids enjoy being the one making this decision. Give them rules of the kind of book they are allowed.

Library and Book Stores are Fun Trips

Story time and games laid out at local stores and library are a fun way to make an event out of visits. Some places even have toys lying around. Give them time to move around, do their thing and then read to them in that setting.

Keep Relevant Books at Home

Always keep a small library at home that is within reach of children. I myself grew up around a ton of books gifted, hand me downs or picked up while traveling. And a big reason that I read is I have always had access to a variety of content.

Have Quiet Reading Time

There is something calming about having quiet time. I have many childhood memories of sitting around with my dad, cousins all of us relaxing after a meal together, reading.

Participate in Local Programs/Challenges

You register, manage a log of the books you read each day and then the kids get a treat at completion. It gives them such a sense of achievement.

Discuss the story

Don't just stop at reading. Use children's natural story telling abilities to turn reading into an adventure. This helps gets their creative juices flowing. Turn the little ones into master story tellers. Ensure they explore the story with questions like -

- What did they learn?
- What was their favorite part?
- How would they change the ending?

Discussing every story they read and the various characters and the many facets of the story helps children understand that within the tale, there is a basic truth being conveyed by the author. This develops comprehension.

Talk about the Importance of Reading

When you explain to a child early how something benefits them, they slowly grow to imbibe it into their lives. The 10 known benefits of reading are –

- Knowledge
- Expanded Vocabulary
- Memory Improvement
- Enhanced Analytical Skills
- Improved Focus
- Empowered Thought Processes
- Stress Reduction
- Improved Cultural Awareness

You can in your own words reiterate these advantages. Reading is a habit, that is beneficial to every single person. To learn a skill, to keep you company or just take a trip around the world from an arm chair!

Strong Roots
For
Good Choices

6. MOTIVATE SELF-RELIANCE

Pampered! That is what I was growing up. For my mom, education was paramount in my formative years. So, if I excelled at my academics and was polite as a person with proper manners, she did everything for me and my extended family. It was only when I became of marriageable age that she would eventually force me to learn how to be self-reliant in household chores.

I never even had to get a glass of water for myself. While this is not something I am proud of, with maturity and my role in motherhood, I understand my mom's thought process. An Indian daughter in law in a faraway country, she was often busy tinkering around the house while the rest of the family lounged around reading books. She worked morning to night taking care of the needs to the many around her, so she felt, "If I'm working this hard for the adults around me, why not my own little ones."

And once she lost everything she and dad had built together during the Gulf War, money became that much more important to her. And in those days, education was the only way to get a high paying salary. It made her drive me more towards school rather than daily life skills. This was true of most kids living in the Gulf around me.

Luckily though, I was born with a "can do" attitude and seeing my parents working hard morning to night (my dad worked two jobs, my mom did many odd jobs too) stuck with me so I was always willing to learn, adapt and work my butt off. It did take me a long while to learn how to; *and that often put me at a disadvantage.*

Teaching Children to Fish

The art of independence comes from knowing that you can do things for yourself. By being willing to learn where you can with a positive attitude. We all wish our kids excel in life. But many of us focus only on the educational aspects of it. Extracurricular activities include dancing, martial arts, singing, etc. whatever will help the kids get into college. But how do you develop the art of "stick to it ness" that takes them there?

The pride one feels in keeping their home clean. The warmth of a home cooked meal. The exhilaration of a taking on tasks that save you money.

A respect for every simple job that exists.

Consequently, I am insistent on imparting basic life skills early.

Getting My Kids to Help Around Home

I made my son help as early as he could walk. Handing me a napkin. Pouring himself and us water. Age appropriate actions that are doable. It was rarely perfect, but the point was to develop a habit.

"Mom!! You always make me do chores. Chores are not to be done by kids.", my son lamented when he could talk. And when he started kindergarten, "What about an allowance for my chores?"

One of the definitions of chores online is - "an unpleasant but necessary task."

We see it on TV and among our friends. Parents say, " Do your chores". The kids whine or expect an allowance in return for doing some menial tasks around the house. No matter what, most of the time there are arguments or nagging to just get them moving.

I realize that the word "Chore" today just brings up negative feelings and responses. There seems to be an inherent expectation of monetary benefit and loss in taking pride in the little things.

Personally, not believing in the concept of an allowance for helping at home, I make sure the kids know the appreciation I have for what they do in other ways. With words, a trip to the book store, treat at their favorite frozen yogurt shop etc.

To that end, we stopped using the word, " Chores". Instead, I say, "Please help out by ... " reminding them consistently. The loss of the word "chores" and expectation of allowance does the below.

Pride in Helping Others

Kids love feeling important. Older. And moms and dads need help. There is no magical fairy coming to do the laundry, loading the dishwasher, making your bed, decluttering or organizing. As a family everyone should pitch in.

The genuine appreciation they receive shows them their actions matter. Everyone contributes depending on the need of the hour. Sometimes, I need help getting the living room clutter free before guests arrive. Other times, I'm sick and need something done that they don't usually do.

Requests Are Fluid

We all have interchangeable jobs, within reason. My son says, "But (…insert name here..) made a mess!" I will respond with, "I help you clean up when you are tired. So, there is no harm in helping clean up anyone else's mess. It is your room/home. Your family." Other times the little one is asked to do her brother's 'job' of putting shoes away or filling a glass of water for someone. This way kids know that they can be asked to do anything. There are no set agendas. You could even write up things to do, put them in a jar and have them pick one when they get bored or a need arises.

Instill Self-Motivation Within

My kids clean up the home fastest when we are having company over. You can see their pride for the place where they have friends over. No job is small or big. Everything you do towards grooming, cleaning or helping carries value. There is much to be said about a home that is welcoming.

Once a circle of pride is established, kids grow self-motivated.

Be Patient

The scenario when I was little: My dad asks me to do something. I'm in the middle of playing out a story in my doll house. He wants it done immediately. I reply, "In a minute!" In frustration, he will go and do it himself. This happened a lot in my house.

I understand the frustration. There are two things wrong with that:

1.We need to understand, kids are also people already doing something. It is unfair to ask anyone to stop what they are doing, because you need something. You don't expect this at work or of adults. You patiently wait for them to finish what they are doing before helping you. Then why can't you wait for your child?

2. If you let it go and do it for them, you lose the opportunity of a teachable moment. No child in the world is going to help by themselves. It takes a lot of reminders and patience before anyone gets around to do what you need done. Anyone who has met a child knows their attention spans are small and fickle. As a parent you need to remember, this is not nagging. You just have to be persistent in making sure they do it.

Do Things Right the First Time

If my kids are grumpy or they do a job badly, in the name of just getting it over with, they not only have to redo it correctly, they must do something else too.

This one important trick gives them an incentive to do everything to the best of their little abilities, the first time round.

Work Need Not but Can Be Fun

Let's face it! These "how do I get chores to be fun?" and constant treats for chores are just in bad taste.

You are not going to find treats or stickers when cleaning up as an adult. There will be no point system or compensation for what you do for your "self". Life is hard. Kids need to know that doing your job need not be but can be made fun by themselves.

- Finding two pairs of socks or jumping in a just washed pile of laundry is can be exciting.

- Talking to each other when emptying and loading the dishwasher builds rapport.
- Helping your mom out by running as fast as you can to get the diaper for the baby is exhilarating!

Finding the silver lining in the mundane is a beautiful characteristic to develop.

Verbalize Your Own Efforts

Every human being naturally takes endeavors done for them for granted. This breeds entitlement when not checked early. Make sure your children are aware of all the hard work you do for their birthdays, driving them around for classes or cooking them a special meal etc. This helps children take that pause to appreciate that what is being done for them carries value.

Gratitude for others' efforts evolves to assessing our own actions, adding to self-worth.

Regularity Breeds Rhythm

By contributing around the home, kids learn that consistency is key. My kids started picking up their toys themselves, at the ages of 7 and 4 with the younger following the older one's lead. The toys were easy to organize with all of them going into marked big boxes.

Habit is nothing but doing something consistently. Yes, it's hard for parents but it is very important to persist in pushing our kids towards perseverance.

If you want something to change, do it regularly. That dedication is a core life quality. In order to grow up into individuals providing value to society they need to know that not every task is going to be compensated for. It is still valuable and needs doing, building character.

Empower your kids with the pride of self-worth.

7. CULTIVATE TALENT WITHIN

Untapped aptitude is such an unfortunate waste.

The desire to nurture a child's talents stems often from our own unfulfilled dreams. We need to help our children discover their strengths, so they can use them in their future endeavors. College applications, part time job to help with extra income. A specific talent may just end up being your child's purpose in life.

It is important for parents to let children develop productive interests outside of academics.

We see so many adults today who spend their down time in front of the television or browsing the phone. While gadget use has its own place in our growth, it is necessary to use our free time to create something out of nothing. Unless we encourage the next generation for this early, it will not come to fruition.

A talent is a wonderful way to feed the soul on days when you feel unfulfilled or low, leaving you refreshed. Huge plus!

My Experiences Cultivating Talent

There are many challenges that one may come across in cultivating a passion.

59

My parents sent me to learn the Indian Classical dance form Bharatnayam at age 4. When I moved to India, I had to change my dance form to Kathak due to lack of dance schools, which I preferred learning for another 4 years. Learning these dance forms taught me discipline, proper posture, stage presentation, being a part of a team, learning the history behind dance in Indian heritage. Dance being something that fed my soul, it made me feel refreshed after a long day at school.

Besides that, I have explored electronic keyboard, Harmonium (Indian instrument), pottery painting, fabric painting & speed typing classes. I have also participated in yoga camps, self-defense camps. The only course which I regret wasting time on was the keyboard playing. With no ear for creating music, I wonder why my parents ever enrolled me, and made me stick to it for a good two years!

Along the way, I have taught dance at summer camps, after school care and choreographed several dance recitals so I am aware of a teacher's perspective as well.

My Son's Extra Curricular Journey

Enrolling my son in a soccer camp at age 3 was interesting. Some kids of course were naturally gifted and had a blast. It was clear on day one my son wasn't one of them. He just wasn't ready. He just stood there. The sun in his eyes. He was confused. He just couldn't understand why so many kids were running behind one ball!?

Frustrating as it was seeing him so miserable on the field, I spurred him on, "I just want you to get some exercise. Just run! Have fun. Move." The result? My sweet child ran around the field aimlessly, with eyes closed till he was exhausted. I of course, did not put him in soccer camp the consequent year.

Till he insisted to be put in soccer again in a local summer camp. The 45 minutes he spent learning were pure joy to watch. As a parent, I learned some children thrive on step by step education. He then went for T ball camp and relished that as well. His swimming teacher the year after did a great job at navigating his distracted energy by taking a genuine interest in his imaginary world.

He joined Tae Kwan Do classes after half a year of pestering me for them. I researched all the institutes in the area and the one I landed on is exceptional for it's amazing coaches. The Masters know just how to get him focused and I can see that he has developed a real interest.

If someone has a real passion, they eventually find a way or I dare say, their talent eventually finds a way to them!

As parents though, a big part of the responsibility falls on us to help nudge our children in the right direction.

Let Your Child Lead

The beauty of talent in any form is that it cannot be contained! Leave a child alone and bored long enough and they will eventually start to get creative. A parent's simple job is to make sure you are looking when that happens and pick up on the cues.

It is also important to find what works in teaching your child a skill.

Your children observe the world around them. Plus, their friends talk. Before long, they will ask you to be enrolled into a class. Follow their lead. It might not guarantee longevity of desire, but it will ensure their effort in trying.

Look for Good Teachers

The right teacher makes all the difference. With many competitively priced sources out there, sometimes it is easy to lose sight of a teacher's relationship with your child.

Judge this instinctively. A good teacher recognizes your child's strengths and uses that to elevate their talent. They appreciate effort and encourage your child to challenge themselves. The wrong kind of mentor on the other hand just does more damage than good.

Explore Varied Interests

Often, I have seen parents enrolling children in classes in which they themselves are interested. While that is wonderful for exposure, it is important to observe if the children themselves have any real interest in the same.

Participating in short camps is an economical way to gauge their reaction to them. If they love it, you can move onto classes. If not, drop it like a hot potato.

Positive Reinforcement is Key

Even the most well-meaning parents do not encourage their children enough. For they assume the child's needs are met at this extra time learning and specially if a child seems naturally inclined towards something.

Don't push them or talk down to them when they do not do well. When they are struggling, find ways to help them. Be their one person cheering squad and coach all rolled in one. Be there in mind and body, yourself.

Instead of taking pictures, look at their performance. Really look! And compliment something they did that no one else in the performance did. That shows you noticed. And that they matter. The appreciation you show right after a performance has far more impact that the one you may show later, while looking at the video.

Right Tools Encourage Growth

Another essential part is providing your child with the necessary tools that they may need to develop themselves. Art supplies, raw materials, a space to practice etc. If affordable classes are not available, lucky for you currently everything can be learned through online videos. Find a way to help your child get the right resources to learn.

Practice Makes Perfect

From a teacher's perspective, I would like to persuade parents to have kids practice at home. Specially if there is a recital on the horizon. Unless of course you have classes 2 days a week or more. But again, if you find your child struggling with an aspect then learn the right way from the teacher and help the child work on it at home.

Do Not Override Teachers

Please do not teach the children your own method or something off the internet. Every mentor has a path in their mind for the student. If you are in doubt discuss this with their teacher. Ensure that the child at no point feels like they must choose between parents and their teachers' way.

Ignore the Whining

Please note, it is hard to get kids to classes even if they love it. Observe whether they enjoy *while* they are in class.

Love it, hate it, the kids will still make excuses. They will feel lazy. They will rebel. They are children. I know it is tedious to take the children to class. And then sit through them. Don't give up and don't let them give up.

There is nothing worse than regret at letting go the path to your passions. If you move or must stop classes for any reason, resume as soon as you can and have the child complete their respective course.

Allow them the space to grow organically within the right structure. Pushing them relentlessly only threatens to remove any passion they have. Finesse takes time. Just because they do not do well once, does not mean they are not learning.

Let them fully appreciate what they truly love doing!

8. IGNITE CURIOUS LEARNING

From walking to talking to academics to sports, we want our children to be achievers. We all have floundered at some point. Yet, most of us secretly hope our children excel in everything they do. It is natural.

Every outsourced academic institute being full of children is the biggest give away to parents wanting their child to be outstanding.

But is this really what we want for our children? Do you want your child to be a straight A student or would you rather they have a love for learning that lasts them a lifetime?

After all, a life of learning takes a marathon mentality. It is certainly not a sprint!

Einstein too, failed miserably in school, couldn't even speak fluently till age 9 and still ended up leaving the world a genius still revered.

Many parents forget that children just like machines suffer from early burn out when pushed too hard, too early.

And that's what happened to me too.

I was an excellent student all through school, which had the curriculum from Indian Central Board of Secondary Education. A totally academic system. I learned 'every lesson by heart' as they say and then poured it all during exams only to have my mind erased of the core concepts for the next year. I was still one of the highest scoring students among all the grades, every year.

Naturally inclined towards excelling, I never really took the time to process what I was learning. My mother worked with me night to day while my other friends would go to tutors. Yet, many of us in Kuwait would have similar lives, school, an extracurricular activity, homework and playtime if it's a holiday. We never developed the joy of learning. I notice the difference when I speak to my husband who has always been a more a hands-on learner all through life.

The only subject I learned diligently all through life is writing, towards which I was naturally drawn. All other subjects just passed through my life with nary a glance.

My mother worried for even that one less mark I would get in a test, and often compared me to the girl who came in second to find out where I had failed. I worked hard because I knew if I didn't, it would make my mother unhappy. That is something I do not wish for my children.

Every child should be nurtured and primed from the beginning to evolve naturally.

That is something I love about the changing education system in many countries. The emphasis is growing on hands-on learning. To teach kids to grow to be self-educators. Even though, the testing has much left to be desired, the preschool phase of encouraging kids' natural curiosity is admirable.

But how do we fuel the same at home?

Encourage a Love of Reading

As we have discussed earlier, it is important for children to be curious about the world and that can only be encouraged through a love of reading. Not to say kids who do not enjoy reading are not curious but reading just opens more doors, metaphorically speaking.

Limited Extracurricular Activities

It is unfortunate when I see many parents send their kids for several extracurricular/academic classes early. Kids spend all day at daycare or school and in the evening are rushing off to learn something else. Every moment accounted for. Weekends are also busy in sports or spent doing extra work when they could be exploring themselves through play.

Kids need ample free play for creative imagination. Of course, they need to learn certain life skills, but it doesn't all have to be at once. Ensure that kids do not get over committed during a week. Provide them with enough time to get inventive.

Let Children Get Bored

The wiling away of time gives little ones a chance to fill it themselves with ideas they have.

I have often been surprised at the many ways in which the kids entertain themselves. Spaceships out of available material. Cars out of pillow cases. Crafting, creating games, puzzles, play acting, even lending a hand around the home themselves when they see me super busy.

Explore the Outside

Understand the importance of playing outside, rain, shine or snow. It is great for their understanding of what wonders the world holds. It helps build immunity and the dirt in the ground is therapeutic. It also helps children develop the ability to be adaptable and curious about how nature works.

Use Online Resources to Your Advantage

Stay abreast of the many apps and video sources out there. These will help you and your child stay abreast of the many wonderful opportunities to grow. Often these can tunnel into your child's natural talents as well.

Make extra effort to consume content about trending topics that today's children are learning about naturally through friends and school. It is a simple online search before you allow your child to play a new educational game that could be potentially harmful.

Encourage Thinking Outside the Box

It happens often. We have had a long day. The kids come climbing on us with their millions of questions and weird ideas and we say, "Just give me five minutes" or "go watch TV". While kids need to learn to respect quiet time, ensure to keep a balance between these two.

Children's boundless questions and talk are germs to ideas that are great for analytical thinking.

Also, don't worry when they start taking things apart. It's a stepping stone to them learning about life's many puzzle pieces and putting them together.

Let kids figure out how to solve problems they themselves create.

Build Internal Motivation

Do not live their life for them. Say it with me.

I will let my child fail as needed.
I will let them make skies that are brown.
I will smile as they make a mess as they create.

Do you understand where I'm going with this? I see it so often during preschool, school projects or competitions I have judged. Work clearly done by parents.

A child that can think of a solution or project for themselves, is much more likely to be a problem solver and achiever than one who is directed to do every single step. Wouldn't you rather your child tried for themselves and failed, rather than succeed with your work now and end up lost in the race of life?

As tempting as it is to reward a child on a job well done, it is important to let them feel the satisfaction themselves. I made the mistake early of giving treats. What it ended up doing is made my son want instant gratification for everything he did. Looking for external validation constantly.

Motivate children to look inwards for validation.

For a child, hey, everything they do is awesome! And it certainly is. But the problem with rewards is children slowly but surely lose the desire to do something just for the joy. They need a carrot to make any kind of move.

A small reward might help you move past an initial hesitation to try something, but then ensure the reward is nothing materialistic. It could be play time or more reading time. Something they enjoy doing, rather than another toy. This is the trickiest part, finding the balance. Something all of us struggle with.

Teach Prioritization

Creating goal oriented, self-driven kids comes from imparting prioritization. They need to learn that the only way to tick a goal off their day is to put it first and put in the work.

Set a time for the target and then get to it.

A neat trick is to tie it into something that the kids love depending on the goal. So, if the goal is something they love doing, they could forgo their favorite treat or activity for that day. And if the goal is something they don't like doing so much, they could get extra time to play or something they rarely get to do within the time period they are trying to achieve their goal. This is something we need to discuss with them in advance. When the idea comes from them, it becomes a lifelong habit.

For example, my kids love watching TV on weekends. But they cannot do that unless they brush their teeth, have their breakfast and do a couple of pre-decided activities before. My son gets to use certain apps only on certain days of the week and gets bonus time only if he finishes all his homework.

Celebrate Small Successes

No, I am not contradicting myself. This balance as I mentioned, is the trickiest part. Kids should learn to do this. Celebrate their own successes in meaningful ways.

Plan a special way to celebrate before they attempt something. Self-driven people know when to work hard and when to celebrate their success and in what way. Preferably an experience vs something materialistic.

Portray a Positive Attitude

Life is not easy. Look at the positive aspects of life, even in the face of self-doubt, fear or failure or just bad days. Self-doubt is inherent in everything we do. No one is born with confidence. And "we know you can do it" goes only a little way.

One of the questions, my kids ask most often is, "What if I don't win?"

It is important to encourage them to push a little harder some days and equally important to know when it is okay to forgive yourself for letting go.

Some of the main questions I ask my kids often is:

"What was good about what you did today?"
"What was a bad thing that you turned into a good thing.?"
"What did you find hard to do today?"
"How do you think you can make it better?"

This simple exercise teaches kids to self-evaluate, problem solve and look at the positive aspect of even a failed attempt.

Meaning of Your Child's Grade

Your child has varied interests. Not every child is going to excel academically. Or in every subject. And that is okay! This is NOT failure in any form. When parents put kids early into extra classes and apply pressure for academics, it makes the child peak and burn out soon. This hampers their future in a way you do not foresee.

What is in fact needed is the teaching of all-round growth.

- *Knowledge*
- *Understanding*
- *Application*
- *Skill*

What a screw is, and its use once taught is understanding. But the actual applications of screw at home and making use of it in day to day life is skill development. How to apply that knowledge is essential. Show children applications of what they have learned in daily lives.

Marksheets are no guide to real life.

Take Time to Understand Your Child

Children are all born a certain way. There is a nature that your child is born with, which needs to be accepted. Your dreams and hopes should not define your child. What needs to happen is for you to take the time to observe your child and take in who they are before molding them into what you think they should become. This is where free playtime, long walks and conversations with your children come in.

Spend time with your child without purpose to better get a sense of who they are.

This is a great tool which will show you where your child is meant to excel in. Do not blame teachers or even your child for not doing well in a certain subject. They just may not be inclined towards it naturally. It's not that your child is not intelligent enough. They just are interested in other subjects and will excel in those.

As you help your child lay the foundation of getting over any fears they have of failure, encourage them to learn a skill because it adds to their character.

9. IMPART SELF CONTROL

The art of self-regulation benefits every single person; in words, in actions and in living.

My parents constantly talked about how important it was to have a balance in everything we do. What we wanted vs how much of it we should be doing/using. When I was little, I never asked for stuff because I knew my parents would never entertain purposeless demands. Yet, it never stopped them from giving me something I really needed.

My parents say, "Kisi bhi cheez ki *ati* buri hoti hai." Translated, it means that *excess* of anything is harmful. An invaluable lesson. Whereas today, kids are constantly lavished with toys, treats, candy on most occasions. Let's not forget fads that grow like wildfire.

One night, I saw an online video of a father posting about his daughter's joy on getting the "latest cool gadget", the Fidget Spinner. The next morning, there were 4 kids at the bus stop spinning them. When I asked why they were taking toys to school, the response was, "They are allowed!"

Not knowing what to make of them, I asked parents around the world online," Yay or Nay" and most parents said, Yay! No one had an answer for why though. Except a parent of a child on the autism spectrum who witnessed their child benefitting from the use as it helped them focus.

A week later though, reports of the same being banned and teachers' requests to please keep the toys limited to recess or better yet home started pouring in. Psychologists came out saying there is no substantial proof to the claims that the fidget spinners improve focus at all!

This phenomenon is not new. A new toy comes into the market, with a cool gimmick attached to it. In this case, "helping kids focus" and before you know it herd mentality of trying the "new thing" and overuse causes the same to become a nuisance.

Herd mentality is perhaps the biggest downfall of human nature.

The same applies to every fad there is. Everyone is following trends without a thought for the actual application. Overdoing it till they cannot do it anymore. I have aunts who have gone on diets that have cost them their health. I know of kids who played video games relentlessly, and today as adults do not know how to be social. Anything in life when done in excess can lead to substantial issues, like obesity, addiction, one track mindedness, health issues etc.

There seems to be an inherent loss of self-awareness of the thoughtful balance we need in life.

Humans are attracted to constant gratification, which can easily allow things to go out of control. Nurturing a basic instinct of responsibility is paramount for success in life and that doesn't just apply to toys.

The crux is to recognize that simple rules or actions like the ones below instill the importance of moderation.

Art of Avoiding Peer Pressure

Sure, kids are getting the latest stuff. But is your child asking for it? Initially, my son said, "It just spins." And then when he did want it because all his friends had it and I refused, he made one himself. I heard of another child who monetized the idea and sold spinners made by him.

When we as parents get onto the bandwagon of the latest trend backing our kids or letting them do something just because others are doing it, we subconsciously preach that it's okay to follow what others are doing even if it's not a good fit.

When in fact, we need to create thought leaders. Lead by example that it is okay to be different and have different choices than those around you, even your friends.

Enforce Understanding of a Trend's Origin

While I am totally in for parents being in the know about what is "cool" to children these days, I draw the line at getting pulled into the wave of blind fascination and needless competition that goes along with it. It is an unfortunate sight to see parents arguing with children about how their child's gadget is better.

If you feel a latest gadget is truly useful for your child, discuss the same with them. Explain why they personally are getting the toy/gadget. What need of theirs is it meeting? This helps them understand what trend to follow and what to leave behind.

Associate Rules with Everything

By this I refer to the fact that when I asked kids why they were taking toys to school, most answered." They are allowed." Even if something is allowed in school, it was the parents' responsibility to understand that, a toy at school would certainly be distracting when most kids were bringing them. We need to ensure that the children have limited use of any one thing. The rules of use can be as simple as –

- Do not use the gadget while in school.
- Do not play with the video game more than x minutes at a time.
- Play only after completing y number of activities.

The same applies to consumption for any kid. Candy, playtime, video games etc. Essential rules and time limits help kids understand that over indulgence is not healthy.

Do Not Reward Tantrums

This bears repeating. You don't want to say yes but they throw a tantrum and say," Everyone has it!" Saying no and hearing them cry, while frustrating is good for their resilience. This specially happens for that new kind of toy or at a restaurant when others are having something that they too want, or a party that they want to go to.

They learn that it is not the end of the world if they do not get what they want, in that exact moment.

Explain Your Process to Spending Money

Children understand much more than we give them credit for. It may seem they are too young for it but understanding the Why of what you as a parent are willing to spend money on gets them thinking of the importance of spending in the right place, at the right time.

My son wanted to go for a party his friends were going to, which had $40 admission per person. I said no. The same day, we ended up going for a festival in which they explored a different culture that had per person entry $20. Our family had a wonderful experience. I explained to him, it's not about the amount but the value of the experience that matters.

Be Conscious About Food Habits

I see so many parents using snacks as a distraction, candy as rewards or stuffing their kids with food, thinking this is essential for growth. Many cultures like the Indian culture, associate love and celebration with food. This often leads to over indulgence.

Self-moderation and eating go hand in hand. When you feed kids incessantly or give goodies to pass time kids miss the opportunity to know when they need to stop eating. Raising mindful eaters is a wonderful way to impart self-moderation since being content in food is synonyms with being content in life. For this –

- Do not use food for comfort.
- Do not give food the minute it is requested.
- Be too controlling where any one food is concerned. A lack of something, instills over indulgence when they do finally get their hands on it.
- Do not encourage or let them overeat, particularly during festivities thinking it happens only once a year.
- Do have a structured day.
- Stay balanced in your outlook towards food. Every single food is a resource in the nutrients it provides.
- Try to avoid consuming empty calories. Build awareness in kids early about sugar, healthy eating and over consumption.

To give you an example, in our home, my kids being cautious eaters by nature, I stopped keeping snacks. No juices either.

Maximum one treat/candy a day, that too rarely. With time now they have come to expect what and when they will get to eat.

Use Celebrations/Family Visits as Teaching Moments

Festivals are a time when things can get out of hand quickly. We tend to desire to make them grand and end up spoiling kids with too many gifts/treats. Like taking one candy at a time during Halloween is more about being considerate to others and building self-discipline.

When my parents visit, they tend to pamper both kids with toys/books, anything their little heart's desire. I understand the sentiment since they do not meet often but during our last visit, I had to request them to limit themselves to fewer gifts so that the kids do not come to expect but rather appreciate the gesture and memory of it.

Discuss Trends and Gimmicks

Make your children world wary. Share with them current stories from around the world. Discuss with them the dangers and positive outcome of each internet challenge, latest gadget, new fad, foods, video games etc. Share your childhood experiences even. This gets their thinking gears moving and makes them aware of moral values, real world consequences and gives them sound directional thinking.

Games, toys and trends have their own place in our social and mental growth but doing anything blindly, just because everyone else is doing it sends the wrong message to the youth.

Nurture your little ones to be self-reliant in practicing core values of moderation.

10. BALANCE TECHNOLOGY

The world of technology is magical. And as with all magic, it too comes at a price. It has seeped into our lives and the fear of overuse of gadget weighs heavy constantly.

We try to be mindful but there is only so much we can do against the high we get from seeing those new message notifications, those points we earn or the desire to stay connected to our circle of people.

Science has established that seeing those red dots, hearing those pings and even watching those series marathons are all akin to drug use. Humans, being narcissistic beings in general love the idea of feeling important or achieving the smallest task, even it is watching another episode of our favorite show. Our brain loves the idea of getting that momentary high of achieving perceived successes, however small.

It boils down to our base desire of being gratified.

Filmy Family of Mine

In India, "filmy" is a term used for movie buffs. People who watch *every* movie, quote movies in real life, watch movies together and use examples of similar situations in real life when applicable. And no family is filmier than me.

My mom's father owned a theatre and every Sunday, movie going was a treat as the family would sit together after and discuss what was to be learned from it and why the protagonist did what they did.

When my mother worked around the house, the TV babysat me. Television watching was not associated with the stress of ratings as it is today because in Kuwait, every single TV show and movie went through a screening process and every scene unsuitable for anyone older than 5 was edited out before release to the public (lovely bubble to live in, I know!).

My mother has always taught me to find the takeaway from any story. Be it a book or movie. There are movies I have watched over 25 times, learning the lessons in it. Not that I only watched TV. The TV was merely the background score to my imagination. I would dance around, pretending to be part of the Sound of Music cast or a heroine in a Hindi movie. And we always, always observed and discussed the moral. Which is why I'm a sucker for every story with a strong life message, however subtly depicted. Even in bad movies.

Life Lessons 101

I would not recommend a gadget babysitting your child. I do however tell everyone that technology is not the enemy. And every single content created has a message and if age appropriate should be watched with kids and the subtext pondered over.

When I had kids, I didn't have much option. With no family close, if I wanted to ensure my kids stayed in one place while I had a bath, the trusted TV babysat my kids for those few minutes. With time, both our dependence grew. The kids enjoyed their shows and I relished being able to have those minutes without "Mom, Mom, Mom ... "

There was always a balance, though. We never sat all day or hours together with television but with the advent of gadgets in my kids' growing years it became very easy it to flit from one to the next. And the total gadget time finally does add up.

Besides that, there is also the danger of the number of apps: educational and otherwise, cropping up when kids talk to each other and then demand the "fun" be downloaded for them too.

Gadget use certainly has some advantages –

- Improved cognitive skills.
- Fun exploring new avenues for kids.
- Great way for early education.
- Better motor skills.
- Sportsmen spirit when playing games.
- More creativity when used in addition to learning.

Gadget overuse has as many disadvantages –

- Hard time focusing.
- Speech or language delay is possibility.
- Being distracted.
- Addiction to device use.
- Lesser desire for real life connections.
- Stubborn outlook on life, since devices are self-controlled, outcome predetermined.
- Less imagination when readymade information is imbibed.

In the world we live in though, gadget use is going to be a big part of our children's lives. So, it is paramount, we set them up for success by providing a balanced perception.

Use gadgets as a tool, instead of us being dependent on them.

Encourage Responsible Use

Every single gadget has its advantages and disadvantages. With man's foray into science, and specially advertising, the pluses are very evident, but every single disadvantage comes into play when you overuse the most useful device as well.

Keeping your child away from any new technology is just depriving them of staying with the times. But yes, imparting them with the balance they need to make better choices is a must.

It is essential to stay in tune with what the world is doing in terms of content. Specially as a parent. Daily you have new trends and pranks being done by kids and more importantly, celebrity driven challenges that affect kids today.

Make sure you go through what's trending on social media or videos that can easily influence young minds.

No Unmonitored Gadget Use

Yes, it's very tempting. I fell prey to it myself in those early months. The kids have the phone/tablet and they keep themselves busy by scrolling from one video to the next.

It started innocently with poems about ABCs. Soon, my son was watching other kids unboxing toys and playing games. It seemed harmless enough, but then he would start crying when we told him to stop watching. The demands for toys grew. One day, while researching I found how some content creators were using kids' favorite characters to talk about inappropriate topics. The kids have not had access to the online videos since.

Be very careful what you let your kids watch. More

importantly, let them watch it on TV. Let the gadgets have pre-downloaded programs that you know are valuable and dear to your kids. Be conscientious in what you give kids access to.

Control Privacy Settings Diligently

Technology is a tool and every tool has an optimum way of use. Staying away from a certain medium might seem like a good idea in the short term but in the long run means your view of life becoming obsolete.

Consider it a necessary evil. Yes, you may choose not to use it at all. Which is one way to go, but if you do use gadgets and apps, be very aware of the many simple ways in which you can control with whom you are sharing your uploads and day to day life.

Decide what works for your family and what rules need to be followed at your home. Talk to your kids about safety and online dangers as well.

Be Careful About What You Upload

People seem to have this misconception, that one kind of upload is safer than another. I hate to break the bubble, but anything once uploaded is going to be on the internet forever.

Since becoming a content creator, I have realized how awful it is when others' use your content without permission. Image copyright and use is a big issue. But the world doesn't think that. There are many who share content without any sense of right or wrong.

Which is why, it is important to be aware of the kind of pictures you upload of your kids. It breaks my heart when I see kids' photos being uploaded that are in the bathroom or on the beach. When people upload candid photos without seeking permission. Other than the kids getting really upset when they grow up (hello! Teenage angst), it is important to remember everything that you are sharing online is forever and can be used against them.

Also, please be careful of checking into locations or sharing your vacation plans with the world. You never know who is watching and may use that information to trick your child or harm you in some other way. I strongly advise people to share life events after they happen and not during. A simple yet effective safety measure.

Be Mindful of Media/Apps You Use

In a world full of content for everyone it is important to be aware of what you and your child are downloading. Research all that you download. Check the age appropriateness, read reviews, check for the catch before using. Is it online or multiuser? How does it enrich your child's life? All questions you need to ask yourself.

Have Device-Free Zones

The best way to model good gadget use is to be gadget-free yourselves. Have device-free zones in your home (maybe the reading nook/playroom?) or plan device-free vacations. A wonderful way to teach kids that one can have fun without devices too. Unplug at least an hour before bed and limit the number of hours you use any given device.

Promote Personal Connectivity

People can very easily use devices to avoid human contact. Instead, use devices to bring your kids closer to friends and family. Talk to grandparents with them, encourage daily conversations with friends. Send art over email/instant messaging. Build a solid foundation for love and relationships. This builds a habit for connectivity. Also, this fosters early the fact that what we say on devices can affect another person who is far away even.

With cyber bullying being rampant, I started talking to my kids early the reach the words you share have and that whatever we put out there should be well thought and socially responsible for it has an everlasting effect.

Set rules around the use of technology -

- Time and type of use is limited per week.
- There is bonus use only under certain conditions.
- There are only certain circumstances in which certain apps can be used.
- No talking to other people over the internet.
- No using devices during social events like play dates, parties etc.
- Outdoor play time, helping around the house and other activities are a must.
- Long road trips are the only time for gadget use in car.
- Be thoughtful in what you say, online even.
- Make sure you follow all safety measures.
- Research and *fact-check* before sharing content with your children and before forwarding it.
- Be aware your child follows your lead in gadget use.

Teaching kids to be aware of these rules early, removes the fear of technology being misused. Today or tomorrow…

Strong Roots
For
Standing Tall

11. INSTILL GENDER EQUALITY

I was an only child till age 10. I was both the boy and girl of the house, never knowing that I was "supposed" to be a certain way. Studying in an all-girls school, I never knew boys to be any different or that I was supposed to like only dolls or pink. Only when I grew up did I start becoming aware of the gap that patriarchy in Indian culture creates between genders. A thought process sadly common in many cultures across the world.

I see it all around me and way too early.

"Boys don't play in kitchen. Here's the train table.", a father says to his two-year-old son.

"Only girls like pink and purple.", says a four-year-old boy when choosing a toy.

"Boys are not allowed in the princess castle.", say five-year-old girls at the park. Parents stand by mute.

The kids learn by example of media or the world. And this has been happening from time immortal. Gender stereotypes were born of a materialistic mindset by corporations further promoted by parents scared of being judged for raising boys "sensitive" or girls who are "tomboys".

With all the sexual harassment cases going around, talk of women empowerment, equal pay, breaking glass ceilings, etc. are we really any far ahead in mindset?

Girls need to be taught early that they have a voice. Boys-that girls have equal rights to making decisions. The simple truth that feminism is nothing more than having a right to choose.

Every human has the right to choose what or how they want to be in terms of their lives. To encourage this all you need to do as a parent is to allow them to, within reason. To explain to them through conversation and action that while every person cannot be equal in every aspect due to varied strengths but that everyone is held to the same standard.

Indian culture traditionally passes on conservative beliefs in subtle ways. Where even today girls are considered, especially by people from my mother's generation 'second class citizens' and expected to be 'subservient to the patriarchy, in any form. It is sad that it is has always been the older women promoting this trait in the name of happiness of the home. There is this silent desire to see every following generation abiding by the rules of the previous one.

Women pushing women to move out of the way of men.

I have seen the other way to be true too. Where women use the word "feminism" to further their personal agenda. When mothers are stoically silent as their daughters keep boys away from play since "boys are not allowed." Where mothers stand silent while their daughters disrespect relationships. When girls stand against men with such vengeance that it seems like being a feminist means hating all men.

These behavioral divisions within generations add up to a crack within the genders in the following ones, creating power plays.

Gender equality is not something that can be handed to a child. It is a balancing act. To teach boys to respect girls and girls to do the same. That everyone needs to be of equal standing. Unless done early, this wedge just grows and leads to less understanding between the two sexes despite best efforts.

Parenting Boys Vs Girls

Let's face it. Boys and girls are as different as the difference in parenting them. It begins from the way you wipe them during a diaper change to the things you teach them, to the way you teach them to do things. How can one generalize boys and girls to be equal when every single child is known to have their own strengths and weaknesses? As a parent though, it is our job to teach our offspring to empathize with others who have different qualities.

For equality belongs to all, and that extends to acceptance of choices one may not understand.

I have often had people tell me how lucky I am for having a boy and a girl. I didn't understand the blessing till recently. My son teaches me to better understand my husband. What a daughter does, is keep you grounded. She makes you keep remembering how it is to be a girl and the trials one goes through to become a woman. That is not to say, without either you are incapable of learning these lessons. It just may take a lot more conscious effort.

You see, often with time, we forget our own pain. And that is one of the foremost reasons many women do not push for gender equality, within their own families or boys. For they forget! I have of course met many mothers of boys who are very empathetic and are champions for gender equality, who are exceptions to this generalization.

How do we impart early this mutual respect?

Non-Gender Specific Chores

Often people tend to say, girls do this, or boys do that. Why not give them jobs that interest them? Or set up chores that are to be done according to age, drawn by luck? In my home, both my kids make their beds, help make whatever food they can, clean up etc.

Be Your Own Savior

Teach your boys and girls early that they must try their best to help themselves foremost. This is not a boy or girl issue or about removing the "damsel in distress" mentality. It is a matter of being self-driven, confident and thus content. When one is happy within, they do not seek to be fulfilled or validated by others. This ensures one brings more to the world when they are older.

No Means No

The pressure we put on kids to "hug grandma "or "give a kiss "needs to be relaxed. Hugs and kisses are precious, and kids need to learn that these should come from the heart.

Affection is a mode of expression. I often see kids forcing kisses, hugs, tickles on friends/siblings. Parents stand by gazing at the cuteness. I agree that the child should not be reprimanded but those are great moments to teach early that when someone says stop, they need to stop.

Accept Differences and Understand Strengths

A boy and a girl are not the same. The idea of feminism is often misconstrued to say that men and women are exactly the same.

Boys and girls have their own strengths. Every being has their place in society.

There are things that boys are naturally good at, as are girls. That doesn't' mean one cannot get better at a skill by practice. It just means, sometimes one just has an advantage over another by design and they need to work harder to get where the other is. And this is something that stands true for us as *people*.

Unless you understand your disadvantage practically, you cannot work on betterment.

Do Not Presume Preferences

Boys like superheroes and girls like princesses. This is a stereotype, sure. But stereotypes have their basis in truth. These days I feel there is a judgement placed on girls to not like pink or princesses for that means they are weak. And boys need to be in touch with their sensitive side. Is this not another kind of pressure?

Let kids like and be who they want to be. My daughter loves superheroes and my son for the longest time enjoyed "girly" shows. That is simply because they took interest in each other's activities. Like all stereotypes, there is nothing wrong is being an exception to the rule or being the rule either.

Ask friends what their child is interested in before birthday parties or give something generic that creates growth.

Look for Empowered Role Models

Find books. Watch movies. A context of powerful people shows your children that every boy or girl can achieve all they set out to do.

Today we have a lot of talk of telling stories of power. Negating earlier stories from our childhood that showed princesses as needing saving by a prince.

Movies now show the princess to be powerful, but often girls are drawn to the old stories. And there's nothing wrong in that. Every princess story has a subtle way in which the princess is strong and that is a wonderful way to promote strengths that are not that obvious.

There is a unique place for the stories we grew up on in teaching children' empathy, kindness, and feeling regal. Every person has a different take away from any story they hear. Why remove one who kind of content from your child's life because *you* believe it to express a certain kind of message?

Besides, we already know what reading stories of brave warriors who have changed the course of history is a great way to emphasis self-reliance

This helps kid understand misplaced biases. Talk to them about what messages they may have received through media content and whether the messaging is right or wrong. Give them the option of figuring out what they want to imbibe within.

Talk through Situations That Might be Uncomfortable

Children love playing pretend. Often, girls/boys like to talk about how someone is a boyfriend/girlfriend just because they spend time together. This is just one example but teach your kids how to respond to such situations. In the above case, I tell my kids to say, "Yes, he's a boy AND he's a friend. I respect him. You should too. "

Bring respect when talking about opposite gender into your vocabulary early.

Another common situation is discussing kissing and body parts. Talk to your kids about their own body when you feel they are old enough to understand. Do not shy away from a conversation. Children are naturally curious. If you do not answer, they will find a resource. And there is no way of knowing how they will process the information they receive from an unreliable source.

My son almost 8 now, talked about finding girlfriends "icky". The conversation naturally led to relationships and we discussed about what it takes to be a good boyfriend and what a big responsibility it is. We talked about the right age I believe is right for the same and how important it is to spend the early years learning and just playing with friends, *as friends*.

If a conversation comes up naturally, address it to their sensibilities, instead of avoiding it altogether.

Do Not Distance the Opposite Gender

Kids are drawn towards their own gender naturally. They simply look towards the older generations on behavior and interest building. Try to encourage playing with a mixed group. This certainly goes a long way in mental makeup and empathy.

My son is still happy to have girls at playdates or birthday parties. My daughter, almost 5 now has best friends who are boys. There is often a girls against boys' situation at social gatherings but that too brings forth conversation about genders and perceptions. Provide a wholesome experience when you can.

Do Not Label Relationships

This might be controversial, but it is a pet peeve of mine. When people say a boy is "popular" if he is friends with a lot of girls or when someone is labelled as another's boyfriend/girlfriend just because they spend a lot of time together. Kids who are young do not really see relationships other than caring or love. To label it removes the beauty of the purity of their thought. It encourages them to label others too.

I tell both my children that while it is great to have friends of the opposite gender, the relationship needs to be respected and cared for.

Be Sensitive to Cultural Differences

Men and women all around the world are treated differently. We see it whenever we are in a diverse group. Subtle differences that your child may question you on. My son for example used to wonder why a lot of Indian festivals involve giving gifts to the girl in the home. I explained to him my understanding of the same, but eventually chose to adapt the celebrations by including them both. Like traditionally, for Rakshabandhan the sister tied the decorated thread for the brother but now in our home, they both tie that thread of promise to each other and give each other token gifts.

When your children talk to you about why the opposite sex is treated differently, take the time to research it and answer them honestly. Try your best to find the origin of the custom or ask a friend who may know, with an open mind. Discuss the same with your child thoughtfully. Do not judge them.

Be Empathetic to Gender Struggles

When we in passing talk about how lucky our husbands are or

make light of the behavior of opposite genders, we teach kids to do the same. Talk instead about how much work a dad puts into his family. Or how moms provide for their children. How some days are tougher than others. Children look up to those around them for how to view the world. Make sure you hold yourself accountable.

Dissociate character traits from gender relevance.

Share responsibilities equally with your partner. Be there for them, as you expect them to be there for you. Don't expect your partner to be the one pampering you. Be the first one to apologize, when you are wrong. Have healthy arguments, away from the kids. You get the idea.

When your kids see you and your partner having a relationship with equal standing, they know their place in their own relationships.

Let the girls be warrior princesses. Let the boys have superhero tea parties.

12. FOSTER FRIENDSHIPS

Friendships are complicated. I learned the hard way later when I was living on my own in India. I had never faced the big bad minefield that the world of friendships can be. I realized how innocent and trusting I was where friendships are concerned.

My parents, a true example of good friends always put their friends ahead of themselves. Stood by them through thick or thin, no matter what the cost to them or their children. My mother's favorite quote is, "You have to give love to get love."

I swore when I had kids, I would teach them to be good people first and foremost, so they never took advantage of anyone. Nor would they fall for people who tried to dominate them under the guise of a relationship.

Today friendships are need and fear based. Most people look at another person and think, "What has this person got that I need. "and the next worry is, "What will this person use me for?"

Is it so difficult to just be there for someone else? Have a good time when you are together, help someone out, share a lot of laughs, a few authentic moments. And just occasionally, put them ahead of yourself, stand up for what's right, and at the very least don't stand by when something wrong is happening.

Say something.

It is. Why? Because most people create relationships with an agenda in mind. And others have been burned so many times that they fear making relationships that could possibly endanger what they have.

Gone are the days of innocent care. People collect friendships on social media with the click of a button depending on the groups or opinions they have in common.

With the number of ways we have available to stay connected, there is no other time that we have been more apart in heart.

We are a judgmental group, us humans. And we are all looking for people to fill our loneliness. But we want our friends to be perfect. Understanding, forgiving of our faults, considerate and unconditionally supportive. Ever present.

We see a crack in someone's armor and use it to brand them. But no person is perfect. Neither you nor me. We all are struggling to make through this juggle of life, intact, protecting all that we love. That means being vulnerable, sharing our joys/sorrows, forgiving others and accepting people for who they are by understanding their version of truth as a possibility.

Being a friend, before we expect another to be one.

It is not possible to have no expectations, but it is possible to have realistic expectations.

My father says, "Every person has good qualities. In order to maintain a relationship, we need to look beyond the bad and keep the good in our minds constantly. To find the person's one redeeming quality and focus on what brought us closer to this person, rather than what we find offensive."

Yes, there will be times when someone keeps walking over the liberties you are providing them, and you will have to cut them off. Unfortunately, the threshold for this seems to be getting lower and lower. Offense is easily taken and acted upon.

Someone shared a wonderfully interesting perspective. She said, "We spend the kids' formative years helping them thrive and letting go of every relationship that threatens their educational time. And when they go off to college, we are left friendless and alone, back to the beginning of building a social circle. This is the single most important reason we need to teach our children to nurture relationships all through life.

Often the stresses of parenting, cause us to be overly judgmental and cynical. It is already so hard to make friends and when we do not handle our relations well, we set a negative example in front of our kids.

Over my lifetime, not having much family to connect to I always relied on friends. This led me to nurture what I had with intensity. Even when upset with them, I would look over the sum of our relationship to figure out how to keep us in each other's' lives. I'm happy to say today, I have the best circle of love surrounding me (near or far), an accepting and supportive constant.

That did not happen easily. I made a lot of mistakes and saw a lot of struggles during my college days when I left the cocoon of my home into a life of independence at a hostel where I learned what NOT to do where friendships are concerned.

It came at a cost of a part of my life, but I learned invaluable lessons I impart to my kids.

Cultural Group Dynamics

Possibly one of the hardest skills to teach a child is how to maintain healthy relationships. We pass on our subtle prejudices to them and thus make them wary of making everlasting connections. It is harder still when you are a cross cultural child who doesn't "naturally" fit into a category.

If you don't already know, let me tell you this facet of society. In their quest to maintain their heritage or sense of belonging they surround themselves with friends from the same language or culture. They don't do this on purpose or consciously even. They do it nonetheless.

Every single culture does it.

And you will notice that children reflect this. Kids of a group of parents (who usually hang out together) will callously, without meaning to, neglect the one person that is not from their group. And it is counterproductive, as it prevents a person from having a rounded-out experience as a human being.

I have been constantly surrounded by people that lived life differently. Yet, whenever asked what was being said or about why exactly something was being done, no one ever took offense and included me in every life event and celebration. It took a lot of conscious effort on our parts to be inclusive of those "different" than us.

Creating Everlasting Connections

It is sad when parents today strive harder and harder to be a part of the rat race that is that politics of friendships. We ought to be better examples for our children. Welcoming everyone we meet into our lives and for lack of a better word, dating them to test out how we fit together is paramount to social growth.

If we don't vibe, we just made a new acquaintance. Not everyone has to be a big part of our lives. Someone once said of me," She has never met a stranger in her life." I find it so apt for what are strangers but people we haven't been introduced to yet. I have always enjoyed meeting people, learning about them to better understand my own self.

For little ones, every single one who plays with them becomes someone they cherish. It's cute. But the earlier you teach them the value of real relationships, the better they learn to thrive. Things parents can do early on are -

- Have playdates as often as possible.
- Take them on daily chores where they talk to strangers.
- Let kids explore experiences with friends.
- Introduce kids to as many diverse groups as you can.
- Teach them early about the below important friendship values.

People are a Long-Term Investment

A person should always be willing to put into a relationship what they want to bring back to them. Find people who are diverse culturally, caring, brave, positive, challenging, thought provoking and above all make you want to be a better person.

You are the sum of the 5 people who you are most in contact with. Make sure these influences are positive ones.

Courtesy Holds Value

I'm a big believer in Thank you and Pleases. That helps a person see what they are doing carries value for you and that you do not take their kindness for granted. Encouraging kids to being thankful for kind gestures instills a lifelong habit of gratitude and expression.

People often tend to take generosity for granted. But we should keep that thin line of formality within all our relationships. Expressing the worth of our relationship often.

Disagreeing is Not the Same as Being Mean

The environment we live in sees parents explaining to kids what being mean is. But I have seen kids quickly equate that to a person not doing exactly what they want or disagreeing with their thought process.

Disagreement is a great way to challenge what you know. To being open to change in thought process. This is a lifelong lesson that is imperative to thriving in relationships and self.

Life is Not a Box but Circles

Our life is made up of concentric circles.

First one has our family, then relatives (if you are close to them), then close friends and then friends and then acquaintances and finally people who you meet once in a blue moon.

The size of the circle and closeness to you decides how much priority and value the person holds. That is directly proportional to your reaction to their actions. Remembering this, often defines beautifully what you are going to do in response when it comes to the circle a person is in.

No is Something That Friends Can Say

I have seen adults flounder with this and something that I imparted to my kids early. That be bold enough to ask anything, (this applies to every relationship), but the person always has the right to say no in response.

You might feel bad about the no, but you cannot hold it against them because there are a million and one reasons a person may refuse to help. It is important you respect the person's decision and accept their assessment of their own situation. Even if you do not grasp it.

Give What You Can, Often

There is a big push on "sharing is caring". I have a slightly different take on this. It is important to let kids be the judge of things that they are willing to share vs the few things that they don't want to.

As adults many people tend to over commit or give things they find difficult to part with. And then hold the taker responsible for taking them for granted or being negligent. Before giving, literally or metaphorically we need to be aware of the risks involved. Commit with awareness.

Give what you are comfortable parting with. When people give beyond their capabilities, and constantly, is when bitterness grows within relations.

Having an appreciation of what is irreplaceable, as in what could potentially be lost or broken teaches kids early the importance of boundaries. Also, that once you give someone something, that thing is potentially gone forever. So, the lesson of being kind just for kindness sake is imparted.

Appreciate People as They Are

Accepting people as they are is easy for kids. It is slowly when they observe us, do they imbibe differences.

It needs to be explained early that everyone is born looking different but have the same insides. When my son first came up with the question of skin colors being different in preschool, I taught him about melanin and its effects. It was a great opportunity to teach him about the importance of skin care as well.

When they see others who "look different" than them, they will ask questions. Answer as honestly and nonjudgmentally as you can. And if you are not sure, find out before answering.

Focus on the Good in People

"Even the worst person has some good in them. That something that people who care about them appreciate.", is something I often heard my dad say.

It is interesting to note how easily kids today say, "I won't ever play with that kid again." or "I don't like that person anymore." The smallest infraction is offensive.

Encourage children to look at the bigger picture. A relationship is a sum of the history shared. It needs to be considered before removing a person from your life completely.

It is not going to be easy, but we must motivate children to let go of imagined or real grievances so that they grow to understand not everything needs to have pushback.

Ask Questions Genuinely

I have always asked my kids to ask about my day and their friends' days. In this entitled world, it is important to be a good listener and learn about the struggles of others.

Never be afraid to ask something with all the innocence of a child. And be open to understanding the answer. Sure, not every concept is understood by kids, but it creates awareness that the world is bigger than them.

The Many Faces of Kindness

Kindness goes a long way in any relationship. And it looks different in different situations. It may be sharing a snack with someone hungry or giving away your candy or asking someone if they are hurt when they fall.

It may also be not calling someone names. Not laughing at them when something embarrassing happens. To make sure we do not label them as others are choosing to.

Being thoughtful goes a long way towards expressing affection. Ask yourself, "What would it take to make someone's day just a little brighter?" That makes for long term friendships.

Authentic Conversations for Closeness

You ask a person how they are, and they respond, "Good". Even when it isn't. Real relation building is based on the foundation of authentic conversations. And how do you teach kids that?

By talking to them and listening to them. By telling them about your day and trying to remember the little things about theirs. Asking them about their friends and the ups and downs of their day. You may say, your child doesn't communicate as much but it starts with you. Talk about yourself and your day. They may not show it, but they are certainly observing the pattern of open communication.

Talk to your kids about being open, about how someone's actions make them feel. Being left out, toys not being shared, name calling, mean words all lead to hurt feelings and resentment carries forward. Teach children to -

- Talk to their friend about what upset them.
- Give the gift of forgiveness when they hear an apology.
- Observe when no repentance is forthcoming after an offence, or if a hurtful act continues. It is okay to walk away then.

Popularity and Being Funny are Not Everything

Give your kids examples of what good and bad friends do. Respect is a big part of any friendship.

No one should let go of old friendships when chasing those who they think are funnier or more popular. Even small kids feel the pressure to be well liked and funny. Talk to them about the responsibility they hold towards those who they call friends.

Playing Alone is Okay

When a child is confident in playing by themselves, they do not desire to constantly be surrounded by friends and thus have the power within them to say no to peer influence.

People have a habit of alienating those who are desperate for company. Other times, there is peer pressure for random transgressions. Thus, it is important to have contentment in self. The balance of self-play and playing with peers. Being alone in a crowded room is possibly one of the worst feelings. Empower your child to know that being alone can have its advantages too.

- Understanding yourself better.
- Being creative and imaginative.
- Exploring the world without bias.
- Being able to stand alone if the time ever comes.
- Knowing when to walk away.

A person who offers true friendship, attracts lifelong relationships that enrich life with memories, growth and joy.

13. COUNTER BULLYING

This girl sat next to me and started talking. We were in the fifth grade, sitting in the school yard during recess. A new school, new people. I thought she was nice to come sit with me. Then, before I knew it, she had my thumb in her hand and she was asking me to agree with her about something. "Say yes, or I will push your thumb back."

I remained silent. And then she started pushing. And my thumb went from throbbing to painful. But I didn't relent.

I don't remember her face or what she wanted me to agree to. But I remember being strong in that moment and knowing then, what would stay with me for the rest of my life. That I would never stand for anyone beating me down. Physically or mentally.

I was 11. I never told anyone.

The older I got, the more I realized there are so many kinds of bullying. Physical, Verbal, Cyber and Relational being the worst ones.

It's when a friend puts you down intentionally constantly, or people you know gang up on you for alleged infractions, or a disagreement causes ex-friends to plan ways to hurt you, that you must stand your strongest. Recognize their actions as spite and not stoop to their level.

Not having lived in India, for the longest time I never understood the subtle intricacies of the cultural hierarchy. It took me a while to comprehend that it was my stand strong nature and not fitting in with the social order, that most disturbed those around me.

Having our kids bullied is one of the biggest fears every parent has. Recognizing those wolves within the sheep's clothes is an essential trait. Specially because so often kids do not want to tell on their friends.

In the early years, it is mostly kids considered friends who commit infractions that border on bullying.

When Your Child is Treated Badly

The first time I experienced this pain, is when someone pinched my 1.5-year-old son. Then kicked him a few days later. Being hurt on behalf of this heart that walks around outside of you is a bigger pain than anyone can imagine. I know the kid who did it, didn't mean to be vicious. Kids often act out for different reasons.

I also know the 4-year-old kid who said to my son, "Your mom doesn't love you." didn't mean it either. He was probably just feeling it himself, needing to pass on the hurt.

These single instances do not add up to bullying but before you know it, you may have someone wanting to keep hurting your child.

Teach your child how to call out someone's bad behavior.

I still remember the time I learned about a child pushing a 3-

year-old down the stairs. The mother was fuming mad! Not because of what the child did to her daughter. But because of what the parents did. Which was absolutely nothing!

What to Do as Parents

It is one of the toughest things to see your child be hurt and worse still to see other parents doing nothing.

There is no *one* quick fix to people who are bullies.

As soon as kids begin spending time together, you see children who do not agree with them. They won't share. They will say mean things. They will pinch and push. They will even show their love in such a way that hurts your child. I have seen kids as young as 3-year-old lie just for the fun of it.

The problem with teaching your kids about dealing with mild - severe bullying early, is before long everything anyone does turns into a big deal. The second someone doesn't agree with them, they get defensive.

Your child will meet every kind of person. They must differentiate between the fine line that separate off hand remarks, disagreements and bullying.

bul·ly1
verb

gerund or present participle: bullying
use superior strength or influence to intimidate (someone), typically to force him or her to do what one wants.

The power is within us all. To give or not to give in to the influence of others.

So, what steps can you take to counter bullying?

Stand Tall as a Parent

The most important thing to remember is that your behavior around your friends is what your child looks to, to understand how to deal with their friends.

So, don't let anyone walk over you. Disagree with people politely. Stand your ground on important topics. And don't let your judgment cloud your vision of a person.

Don't let your negative relationships influence your child.

Respond Coolly to Mean Comments

What someone says is their perception. It is not the truth. Most often they are just projecting. And a reaction just enables them. Let the words bounce off your being.

You are loved. You are special. Nothing could ever change that.

Just agree with the person in question. It instantly takes away the power. Saying "You are right" or "That's your opinion, not a fact. ", is a great response.

Indifference is known to be the best way to get under someone's skin.

Physical Altercations

Tell your little one to get away from the person in question. Get an adult. Let your child know you stand behind them. Let them know if it happens more than once, they are free to retaliate in whatever way they feel comfortable. I know we are often fearful of how kids will ultimately react, but it is important for kids to know their parents have their back in such times.

I see mothers who say, "It's okay when the kids rough house. Kids will be kids." The same parent will throw a huge fit when their own child gets hurt. Therefore, convey to them early that your kids do not "rough house". Let parents around you kindly know about the limits you have in your home.

Friends and Bullying

This is the hardest lesson to teach young kids. They love completely and truly so it is difficult for them to comprehend when someone they care about puts them down.

Teach your kids that sometimes even friends do wrong things. Good friends respect you. Treat you nicely. Other times, friends are just having a bad day. So, it is important to just forgive and let it go.

But, if a friend is hurting you again and again, that person is surely not a friend. I was heartened when my son chose to stop going to parties where there would be a child who would time and again demean him under the guise of being a friend. I have seen girls pinch and pull my daughter's hair and become innocent when their parents come into the room. You will note such children deny any wrong behavior, when questioned.

Teach your child to say out loud, "You cannot ... (say this / do this) to me... "or immediately go and complain loudly to the parent. So, everyone in the room is aware of what has just happened. This is especially useful for parents who tend to ignore their child's bad behavior.

Prevent Your Child from Hurting Another

I explain to my children again and again that if you hurt a person, you don't just hurt them you hurt everyone who loves that person.

It is important to remember that not everything friends do together is funny. If you and your friends are laughing and even one other person is crying, upset or angry, then someone is not having fun. That means something is not right. That they should always be careful of what they say to someone.

We need to teach our kids the social cues to look out for when they are behaving outside of home. They need to understand the consequences of their actions and of the fact that you will not stand for them being hurtful in anyway.

It takes very little for a child to become a bully.

- Personal aggravation. Externalizing internal issues.
- Lashing out when they feel hurt.
- Desire to fit in with other friends.
- Wanting to feel older.
- Feeling jealous or envious of other's having things, attention even.
- Making light of another's attributes just to be funny.
- Mimicking parents' aggressiveness.

Remember, a lot of bullies don't understand that they are being bullies.

It requires a lot of introspection for anyone to look towards their own actions and owning up to them.

Talk to your child about all the above and how to avoid these pitfalls that they themselves could easily fall in.

Standing up for Friends and Family

This is a heartening way to make sure you child starts to develop a protective attitude. Talk to them early that a person should stand up for their friends and family. Especially siblings.

My daughter is blessed that all my son's friends adore her but there are times when they too hurt her or her feelings. My son instantly puts his foot down.

Another day my son came after school and informed me that all friends had climbed on top of a friend. He immediately realized it and stopped. But try as he might he couldn't get his friends off. He was miserable.

I told him he did well to choose wisely but next time to not just do what everyone was doing. As to how to help that friend, he should have called an adult. Often to save someone, you must stand against your own friends. And that's okay too.

Question Your Child's Motive

We as parents have a blind spot where our kids are concerned. Often children say things that aren't true. The source of this lies in many factors. Not to say that the child is bad but maybe they are experiencing feelings they cannot verbalize in the right way.

When your child says something, take the time to think about what they are saying. Ask probing questions and calmly try to understand what your own child's version might be relaying to you. Schools and play dates see children driven by different environments.

A child experiences varied emotion in environments away from home and thus they tend to be a version of themselves parents do not often see.

Before taking any rash decision based on your child's words, understand what might have happened. Take time to get the full story.

And in case of conflict, converse with other parents instead of lashing out.

What to do After

It has happened. Your child has been hurt or has done something that is looked upon as bullying. What do you do after?

Teach your kids to be quick with action and apology. And also, to be gracious in their forgiveness.

What we should impart is –

- Treat others with respect and kindness always.
- What you are experiencing does not give you the right to treat others badly.
- Good behavior harbors good will. Bad brings back bad wishes from others and those who love them.
- Bringing attention to someone being treated badly or someone who is hurting another in any form is *not* tattling.
- Bullies need to be ignored but after the 3rd encounter need to be shut down ASAP. The longer you put up with it, the more powerful they think they are becoming.
- With people, body language matters. When confronting someone – maintain eye contact, stay calm and use the bully's name, loudly calling their behavior out.

As we teach our little ones to stand up for themselves and others, slowly we lay the groundwork for a kind world.

14. BEWARE OF PREDATORS

I am neurotic about predators. When my children go for activities, to the park or for classes, I'm constantly on the lookout for people who may not be *safe* or are *over-friendly*.

The first time I was assaulted was at the age of 11, in Bhopal, India. The postman, took my hand, placed it over his pants and then kissed it through the iron gates that were between him and me. Luckily my rapport with my mother meant I immediately went and told her. But the many times after in various cities, in transportation, on the roads, now as a mother leaves me reeling with fear.

I don't share this to scare you.

Similar events taught me at an early age, that there are many deranged people out there. The most important thing is to have that open line of communication where we know our children will know what to do when they recognize it and come and tell us promptly.

While being molested are some of my worst memories, in some ways it made me hyper aware and stronger. I unfortunately also got desensitized to it all. Not a good thing!

The normalization around the world about sexual assault across cultures stems from many reasons but foremost the acceptance that this is something that happens to everyone. Whenever women sit around, these stories are shared like battle scars and in the same breath we pray this never happens to the next generation. But are we doing enough to prevent it though?

Consequently, I'm a strong advocate that the conversation begin early so that children know to respect the opposite sex and be able to recognize such behavior, understanding that sometimes even people you know are capable of horrible acts.

I started talking to my son about personal safety when he was 4. Daughter 3. Specially because they both are extremely friendly kids. This makes them easy preys, should someone choose to take advantage. On the other hand, I never want them to lose their happy demeanor. To be too scared to say Hi to strangers.

We need people who are friendly to make the world a loving place to live. Who aren't scared to be the first one to break the proverbial ice.

So how do we create a balance of awareness and safety?

You will find it useful to use the below as baseline to start a dialogue essential for proactive thinking. To start talking about this disturbing topic is the first step.

No Secrets Within Family

When they are young, they are to know that it is wrong if someone, specially an adult tells them to keep a secret.

My parents have always had open dialogue. There's absolutely nothing I feel uncomfortable talking to them about. This, I think is what helped me just go and tell my mom, "The mailman took my hand and put it on his pants." immediately after it happened. One should never feel hesitation in telling their parents anything.

I always say that no topic should be barred from discussing with kids, especially when they see something on TV (adults kissing) or hear something that may possibly confuse them about issues. Listening and letting them ask questions, no matter how uncomfortable, that are answered as you may see fit is a great way to make sure kids trust parents.

Your Affection Carries Value

No one and I cannot emphasize this enough, *no one* should touch them inside their shirt or skirt/pants. Or kiss their lips. With some people being extra cuddly, it is okay that kids understand that saying no if they feel uncomfortable is just respecting their body.

This is one of the reasons why I too personally always ask children for hugs and kisses. They can always be taught to show their respect and love in other ways. It means a lot more when it comes from their little hearts anyway.

Permission is Must

We tell our kids they have to ask before going anywhere but many a times we forget to tell them not to walk off with a friend to an unknown place. They should always play where you can see them, and they can see you.

They should understand walking off into the horizon behind a balloon or ice cream cart is not okay. Going to a secret exciting place with a friend or some adult they know is not okay. They should always ask for permission from the person in charge before going anywhere.

118

Define Strangers

In the beginning, when I started this conversation my son asked me, " Who is a stranger? ". We went on to discuss who all are considered family. People who we trust immensely. We also went over those we just meet once in a few months, explaining they are a part of our outer circle.

It is important that kids understand the definition of a family's boundaries. My kids often ask if they can talk to strangers. I respond, "Yes, you can talk but you cannot go with them or help them."

No Helping Adults Alone

It's important to be nice. Say hi to strangers. Smile at them but remember to explain to your child that they are too young to help an adult. Many children feel very grown up in being able to do something an adult asks them to do.

They are in a constant hurry to prove themselves or please others. So, if an adult who is an acquaintance or stranger says," Can you help me with ... " / "I need help in this room ..." they are to respond with, " Let me go ask my parents/teacher first. " or just run away if it feels unsafe.

There is Enough at Home

Kids are greedy by default. It's is human nature. They are drawn to that extra piece of candy or toy or whatever is their favorite thing. And many times, we parents exploit this honest response by making lot of activities incentive based. (another reason I'm against material incentives)

Every child needs to know that their parents can provide everything for them. They do not need to ask or take anything that any other person offers them in return for something.

And all this bears repetition, constantly. For kids to understand all that there is to be aware and steps to take if the situation comes. To be so aware that they can sense danger from a mile away.

What to Do When You Feel Uncomfortable

Run away, Shout and Assault

Running away is the best policy in any dangerous situation. Their first response should be to shout out and run away.

As parents, we tell children hitting is not okay. But if someone does grab them then nothing is off limits. Nothing! You can hit, punch, bite, scratch and most importantly scream. We even practice the volume level and bite/kicking at home.

Read Books about Icky Feelings/Bad Touch

There are some wonderful books that help teach kids early about the uh oh feeling or what to do when someone tries to grab your hand or lure you away.

Fear is not the solution to anything. The world is scary. The only way we can live is being constantly cautious. As adults we now are naturally so but we need to enable our children to do the same and know what to do in any given situation.

Arm your kids will tools of awareness. Teach them the difference between strangers and predators.

15. PREPARE FOR TRAGEDIES

We lived an idyllic life. My small family thriving. Dad doing two jobs. My brother just born and me a ten-year-old busy in a child's life.

Till the morning of August 2nd, 1990. When Iraq invaded Kuwait. And the Gulf War ensued.

We lost everything. I was ten. The impact of the loss of all our materialistic possessions and many of our relations (in the aftermath), affects me immensely today. After I have a home that I have put together painstakingly with my husband. Every item in our home has a purpose and a story. My parents lost 10 years of their life in that war. Even photographs, memories all gone. I shudder to think of us losing all we have.

When I read headlines of mass shootings, my throat constricts. My heart beat stops. I look at the number of people who died, and my eyes well up.

There has been a vicious cycle of despair recently. Hurricanes, acts of terrorism, mass shootings have left families reeling under the possibility of tragedy slamming into their lives at a moment's notice.

Lost links. Hearts broken. Lives changed forever!

Highly sensitive people like me, especially those who have experienced loss earlier and now are parents, imagine themselves in that situation. We constantly look over our shoulder, anticipating danger. Prepare for what we would do, should we feel threatened. We scour information for how to try to stay safe and avoid public places that might be an easy target.

For acts of God, we make endless lists and prep our homes for eventualities. How do we prepare our children though?

Harsh Reality for Kids Today

After the first mass shooting, my son told me about a drill they do now. He explained to me what they would do if a "mean man" came to the school wanting to do bad things. We don't watch the news in our home. So, I don't think he yet knows the actual implications of what the drill prepares him for. I'm constantly petrified at the thought of him and his friends ever having to go through that in reality.

What a sad world we live in where we need to prepare our kids for such circumstances! But taking the school's lead, in spite of how nauseous the thought makes me, I have to prepare my kids to the best of my ability.

Have a Code Word

If your kids are anything like mine, they do not listen to anything you have to say easily. Talk to your kids about a word they think denotes urgency and that puts them on the alert for instructions to come.

Prepare a Simple List of Instructions

I'm a big believer in preparation. Make sure your kids know to run, hide, or do whatever it is that you ask them to do. Every child is different and needs a different set of instructions to follow. You know best how much your child can process. At school, kids mimic other kids. At home though, it is up to parents to gauge what detail of information your kids can process.

For example, in my home I say the below to my kids.

- Listen to what mom dad or an authority figure says.
- Stay with mom and dad no matter what.
- It will be a very difficult situation so stay very quiet and listen hard.
- There could be situation where we say Run then RUN!
- If mom and dad are not there, call so and so and ask for help.
- Find a person in uniform and tell them your address and phone number.
- Both my kids know how to use the phone and numbers to call in emergencies.

Teach Them the Meaning of Emergency

Different emergency situations call for different reactions. What a need is in case of a natural disaster, health emergency etc. You can prep a bag with bare necessities and emergency care that they know where to look for.

Discuss Dangers and Environmental Issues

Let your child know in general, and as they grow scientifically what each one is and how basic tips on how to behave. My kids are super friendly. It has been a hard journey teaching them about how to figure out what a bad man does and how they should protect themselves.

It is even more difficult to explain to my fear filled son that a tornado is not something that comes randomly with every rainfall. Explaining to him the nature of weather and how hurricanes and other natural disasters occur, has been helpful.

Reiterate the Above Frequently

Like everything else in life, this too needs practice. So, ensure to make your kids understand that the above is important and needs to be remembered.

Utilize Time with Kids

These are difficult times. More than anything, kids need to know they are safe and loved. My kids are sensitive so even when we talk about monster men or bad situations, they get disturbed. With information coming in from all quarters even if you protect your child from the media, they may have friends who talk to them about real events.

Snuggle time or walks are usually when kids share what they have been learning outside home. What their friends have been talking about, things that freak them out etc. Make sure to be present with your kids to stay connected to what's going on in their little hearts.

Have open lines of communication always!

Be Proactive for Positive Change

Rather than worrying about a problem, try to be a part of the solution.

Kids are always observing and pick up on body language cues. While it is impossible to be positive all the time, we can teach kids to be empowered by being great examples ourselves. We need to hold onto hope and light the candle for our future generation.

- Volunteer as much as you can.
- Have open dialogue about mental illness, drug use etc
- Surround yourself with positive energies.
- Fact-check before sharing content with others.
- Go over how your family can help someone else in times of need.
- Do your part in being environmentally conscious.

Above all, ensure to do everything in your power to be a kind human being yourself! Do give your kids an extra tight hug on the disturbing days.

Strong Roots
For
A Global Mindset

16. INFUSE YOUR HERITAGE

Growing up, we visited India a lot. Once every year for 3 months, my mom and dad would pack up 45 suitcases (certainly felt it to a kid!) and we would travel India visiting our numerous relatives for a couple of weeks each. It was always great, enjoying with my many cousins but I never complained about going back home either.

You see, for me that was all it was. A visit.

In India, people talked differently than what my life was. I listened and accepted it on face value because I was a kid. They spoke about their life in absolutes and my life in Kuwait while different, was my "real" life. i.e. studies, friends, dance and the freedom to eat non-vegetarian food to my heart's content, away from judgmental eyes of the part of my family that were vegetarians.

I went to the Indian School in Kuwait, all our family friends were Indian, and we went to India during vacations to visit family. The only seeming differences between India and my life in Kuwait were the amenities.

But there was a clash in subtle differences in thought between Indians in India and outside. No one would admit it, but it existed. It's not that either considered themselves less of an Indian but there were subtle nuances lost to me that were obvious to others inside India.

Like the very first time, after I moved to India in 1990 during the Gulf war, when a kid on the school bus asked me, "Where are you from?"

And I said innocently," I'm from Kuwait."

She shook her head. "In India."

I didn't understand her question.

She reiterated, "No, where is your family from."

"Oh, my dad is from Gwalior and my mom is from Maharashtra.", I said.

"Love marriage.", the kid grinned.

"No", I thought feeling weird. "We are Rajput by birth. It was an arranged marriage. My mom's grandfather settled in Amravati, so they have been there since ages."

That conversation has haunted me time and again because that is the very first time, I was asked to explain who I was. I'm grateful my mother never shied away from discussing everything about her and our family with me. The fact that I could answer with conviction made a huge difference to my confidence.

But that was certainly the first-time I understood how important it is for others to know who a person is, defined by where they are from. Even 10-year-olds.

As a child though, I never questioned me being Indian. All I was, was Indian. I didn't know there was a difference in the kind of Indian you are perceived as.

Yet, in no way did that ever negate the pride I feel about being Indian by birth. I stayed connected to my heritage through visits to India, conversations with my mother and joyful celebrations with my family and friends. Each celebration for me is not just a series of rituals; it brings forth fond memories of laughter and love.

But like many of my friends who grew up in Kuwait, I consider it my home. Despite not being a Kuwaiti citizen and in this day, not ever being able to go back there, my heart warms whenever I read or hear about that country.

Empathizing with My Son

Which is why I totally understood when my son used to say, "Mom, why do I need to wear these Indian clothes for festivals? My teachers don't, and my friends don't. And anyway, I am American." He would rather wear a normal t shirt and jeans to every celebration.

I had to explain repeatedly for a couple of months that because his parents were born in India and brought up in Indian culture, it will always be a big part of his life. Also, it is respectful to dress up as needed at any function. It's like having a theme to a party.

No matter where you are now, being aware and respectful of where you came from is equally important.

As parents, we need to understand what it means to have children who grow up in a multicultural society.

Share Childhood Stories

My mom would often tell me about how life was when she was younger, time spent with her grandmother. It helped me understand why things were a certain way.

Share parts of your life and history with your child. It is wonderful when their eyes light up with what was and how different life is.

Read them stories from their own culture. They often mirror how life is. Not in totality, but a lot. Explain to them the evolution of their heritage and your experiences learning about self.

You may think they are young, but they grasp much more than you give them credit for.

Do not Hang on to Just Your Heritage

Anything when held on too tightly, eventually slips out of our fingers.

I see it happen way too often. For fear of losing their identity, parents emphasize too much on their own customs and culture within the home. Exploring only the "fun" parts of other cultures. Not really teaching the learning lessons within them.

Eventually, as the kids grow, they refuse to accept things blindly as their thinking develops over time. Our children are growing up in a time and place totally different than our own. But we need to accept that they are not just part of our heritage, but one which is almost alien to us.

To understand their world, first we must accept the duality of our lives. We originate from and are surrounded by another culture. This should be reflected in our experiences and explored in our actions.

Celebrate Life Fully

Make the effort to rejoice in the little things unique to your culture and share traditions with your children.

A lot of customs are getting forgotten due to lack of time. While I mentioned above not to hold on too tight, it is also seen that many people just forego their own culture in favor of the one surrounding them. An equilibrium is needed. Unless of course you have chosen to consciously remove certain traditions/rituals.

No matter how small or big the celebration, make the time. Create your own family traditions. Donate and volunteer your time every festive season. Connect with your community in those days. Make the time to introduce the people around your life to the festive atmosphere that is within your home. The warmth has the potential to be carried forward generations.

Explain Reasons Behind Customs

A big part of why children move away from their culture is because they cannot connect to it. They find the customs or superstitions outdated. Make sure you understand the origin and reasoning behind all that you do. The advantages are two-fold:

- Your child can relate better and take pride.
- They can carry on the rituals knowing the reasoning, even educating others.

Adapt with Time

To be fair, many customs *have* lost the reason that they were created for. Science has taken leaps and bounds. Make sure you adapt your beliefs to the times you are living in so as not to have your children leave everything behind. The reasoning, "We do it because it has always been done this way.", wears thin.

Meet Family Often

Cultures are carried forward by the emotion that is hidden within them. While it can be hard to spend x amount of money traveling back and forth, arrange for your family and you to celebrate the major holidays together so that you all can learn about the little traditions you each share and grow together. Use gadgets to stay connected and spend special occasions together.

The bond your children build with extended family is one they will cherish as they grow.

Encourage Native Language Speaking

Early acceptance of the mother tongue makes for easy learning of languages. If not done early, it just takes a lot of time and patience. Language learning is a wonderful way to connect with any culture since many words give an insight into how people think. Connecting with your people in their native language is instinctive.

Do NOT Belittle Your Home Country or Heritage

Many people tend to put down their own culture when they look down upon how their country is run or lack of amenities etc. Being disrespectful of any culture is bad but putting down your own heritage is detrimental to your child's acceptance of their heritage even at a young age.

Teach Them Pride in Every Aspect of Their Being

I have seen it happen a lot at cultural events. They celebrate Indian culture in all its glory. Forgetting to address the fact that the little ones are as much Indian as American. It is important for us to teach the kids to respect every culture that makes them who they are. And I believe this should be instilled early in children.

To have as much respect for their parents' homeland as well as the country where they live. For both play a bit part in the development of a person's essence.

17. CELEBRATE DIVERSITY

The more I spent time with people from other sub-cultures of India and cultures around the world, the better understanding I had of what I appreciated about my own culture. I imbibed many things from the worlds I experienced and the rituals within my home evolved.

Today, my heart is filled with gratitude for every home that opened their doors to me, including me in their celebrations, meals and conversations. It helped me have such a unique understanding of how the world works and my own self too.

Yes, your heritage is important. But the world is so big, and we are but a fraction of what it encompasses. Today, when we share bits of the globe with our child, they carry forward lights within them that create a ripple of love and happiness that will last forever.

Do You Suffer from Cultural Blindness?

Cultural Blindness is the inability to understand how some situations may be seen by individuals not belonging to that culture due to one-dimensional perception, values or thought processes rooted in their own cultures. Four Causes of Cultural Blindness are:

- Getting very involved within our own stressful lives.

- Falling prey to targeted social media that only strengthens our singular opinions.
- Not being able to travel as much as we would like to.
- Consuming content only from one culture.
- The fear of losing our heritage and traditions.
- Lack of conscious effort to have conversations outside our comfort zone or with other cultures.

Not everyone lives in multiple countries, and those who do not, need to be especially mindful of succumbing to cultural blindness.

Each of us lives in a sort of cultural bubble – a comfort zone that gets formed due to our current environment. It is made of age, place, and most importantly life experiences. To widen this bubble for our kids we need to share with them that there is more than one way to view the world.

It is essential to explore all that is outside in order to better appreciate what is within.

I celebrate Thanksgiving and Christmas with as much enthusiasm as I do Holi and Diwali. Since I was a child growing up with Christians next door, Christmas was always the highlight of the year for me. The warm vision of their celebrations dance before my eyes even today. What is life but a series of moments. Isn't it wonderful if we can find ways to enjoy most of them?

How Do You Explore Diversity Around You?

It is difficult. With parents being tied up in minute to minute activities of children and work, one must make the effort to seek out multicultural experiences if you want your family to grow in thought.

Actively Seek Diverse Books

Today, multicultural books are sprouting around the world at a fast pace. More diverse authors are making their perspective known. There is no lack of representation any more. You just need to look.

Read articles that originate directly from the country or culture you would like to learn about and keep the lines of dialogue open with your children. Help them find similarities and compare differences to their own lives. As a family, explore the other country's cultural values and traditions. You just might find something new you can all implement together.

Visit Various Local Festivals

Every community today wants the world to know about their cultural heritage. They want to share their traditions and foods to build awareness about their part of the world.

Capture the opportunity by finding local festivals near you that helps foster a love for new country and lifestyle.

Travel to Out of the Box Locations

While it is fun to visit popular travel destinations, find new cities to explore. Traveling is expensive (whether within our own country or to foreign countries), and most parents can embark upon new adventures rarely. To parents who are financially fortunate enough to occasionally manage some travel for your families: please seek out more than just the "main attractions".

Make sure you see the "real" side of the location you are traveling to. Talk to the locals and find the places they think represent the area best. Experience the culture in its totality.

The further you go from the tourist attractions, the more authentic your experience will be.

Celebrate Festivals Not from Your Own Culture

I am a very strong believer in celebrating life to the fullest. Even the smallest celebration can be marked with a memory. If not a big party, then a family dinner with a unique theme. When kids see us making every occasion festive, they slowly begin to enjoy preparing for each festival with you.

Last year I wanted to celebrate the Chinese New Year. What did we do? Watched videos of the origin and cultures, made paper lanterns and ate Chinese food. That week, we read a few books about Chinese history as well. And now we have a new tradition.

Many preschools/schools today explore diversity along with the kids. But do not leave the onus on the school only. The reason I say this is because when kids see parents not doing something they are being made to do, they lose interest in learning about it quickly.

Watch Kid Appropriate News/Documentaries

This may seem simple but the search for diverse content suitable for kids or even content that helps them better connect with the world is hard. We are so busy consuming content from our own culture, we do not think to go out of our way to find diverse media. Usually we are so school curriculum driven that we miss out on what is happening today and how it affects us.

Culture specific documentaries, kids shows etc. are a great way to get started.

Find Origin Stories of Celebrations Around the World

Each celebration brings forth great teachable moments and lovely lessons of life, history or mythology, when delved into deep enough. If all you do to celebrate is bring home a book about the story of origin or how it's celebrated around the world, your lives will be enriched.

You can search online or go to the local library and talk to a librarian. Also, you get the bonus of adapting a new tradition into your family, which is super fun!

Explore Foods Together

The best and sometimes, most adventurous part of any culture is their food. Find out what is the authentic cuisine of a culture. For example, Indian food seems to be limited to Tikka masala around the world. But it has so much more to it than that. Indian food is as diverse as the number of languages spoken within the country. Ask friends from a different culture, what they would recommend for you to try out if you are ever in a restaurant from their culture. Make sure to ask for the proper name of dishes you try out at friends' homes.

Cooking with your children, exploring new recipes/restaurants is a wonderful way to give children an entry way into a multicultural cuisine.

Learn New Languages

As I work on teaching my kids their native language, I encourage them to learn ASL, Spanish and French too. We are learning frequently used words together and it is enriching to learn of the many ways in which words are pronounced. It is interesting to note how some words run common through cultures.

Look at the Globe

The globe is an adventure within itself. Where you can instantly learn about new places. Pick a place a week and find out more about it. Maybe plan an imaginary trip or just look at pictures of what the city represents. A fun activity to teach kids about life all around the world.

Talk to Friends Honestly

I have noticed some amount of misrepresentation of culture within digital media, which seems to be a major source of cultural information for people. Instead talk to people. There seems to be this inherent fear of offending someone. If you have a question about religion even, ask. Instead of passing on your incorrect presumptions to your children, be open to learning. Most people love sharing their life. You just need to be open to listening.

I do hope in my heart that as my kids explore the world, they find what traditions work for them and incorporate the best of everything they experience into their lives.

18. MANTRAS FOR TRAVEL

Shuttling between India, Kuwait, USA and the many cities in between over a lifetime can teach a person something about travel. The time spent visiting family will forever be etched in my mind. Fun with cousins, visiting new places, the *misadventures* even have become anecdotes I talk about often.

Today, there is much ho hum around traveling. It is like a major undertaking that parents get super stressed about. Everyone worries about how to make a trip extra special for kids. When I was a child, the trip was *the adventure*. No one gave us gadgets for entertainment or carried our stuff or made special trips to kid friendly locations for us. We were expected to toe the line - looking out the window, taking breaks when everyone did, making the most of the trip anyway we could.

That's the thing about kids we do not foresee. We worry more about their comfort than the advantages traveling provides them.

- Being brave and adventurous – New experiences are often scary for kids. Trips give an opportunity to explore unknown facets of themselves.
- Developing Resilience – Travel takes patience and certainly a lot of adaptation on the move. This teaches kids not everything goes our way and that's okay. We

just need to go with the flow.

- Entertaining Yourself – Long flights and drives are a great time for kids to learn how to entertain themselves. A quality much needed in every adult's life.
- New learning experiences. – Of course, every adventure includes encounter with different ways of living and things to do. Once experienced these give a better sense of life.
- Conversational techniques – Talking to people from varied backgrounds is a great way to develop communication skills.
- Being responsible – Taking care of themselves or things assigned to them and following the many rules needed to be safe motivates a huge sense of responsibility.
- Developing faith in the world. – When you see people in different environments being nice to you, it surely helps you develop a non-cynical view of the world in general. A quality much needed for a kinder generation.

Early Travel Days with My Kids

The first time I travelled by air with my son, I prepared for 2 months before the flight. Flying alone all the way to Kuwait with a 1.5-year-old was terrifying for a new mom. I asked every person willing to share their experience to advise me on how to have a smooth flight.

I learned a lot about travel but more importantly the experience made me empathetic to other moms' plights as they struggle to change diapers/clothes or feed on flights, neither of which are easy. A few more trips and we thought we had traveling with little ones down, which is why we traveled earlier with my little baby girl.

Traumatic though is an understatement for the flight we took with my 6-month-old, three years later. She cried for 3 days straight and refused to recognize my husband. Which led to both of us having cramped hands. Me holding her in my arms, him from holding my hand up as we walked the lengths of the airports. She proceeded to have a 2-week jet lag on a 3.5-week trip with me sitting right next to her every waking moment. Was it worth it?

Of course. The kids bonded with family and created memories that will last us forever. I have the photos to prove it.

The many trips after, have never been easy either but it is the journey that is the adventure. The memories at the destination are just the fruit of the labor.

So, how do you prepare for travel with kids?

Travel Mantras to Keep in Mind

Ignore the Elephant in the Room.

Your child will cry. Yes.

Believe me when I say this to you *Most of the people are NOT judging you.* I say most because sure there are those whose ideal world hasn't yet been transformed into beautiful chaos by a child. And there just might be a few people who have had a bad day themselves, who just want some tranquility and wish they were … well, anywhere else. You really cannot blame them!

But the major demographic is of people who care about You. They feel for you. They are those who would happily come over to you in a heartbeat and offer you tips, advice, any help or even hold your baby for a minute if you would let them.

They all get it

They all have been there. They have had new born kids who are now older kids with issues that now seem far more difficult to deal with. They may in fact even be missing the simplicity of a crying baby. Ha! Just a baby who is new to the world, who doesn't understand what is wrong and is expressing in the only way they know how to. And this is true across all cultures and countries. (btw, this is true of restaurants, social gatherings and other situations as well.)

My heart thanks the lady on my traumatic flight to India who gave me her child's toys to soothe my baby to maybe distract her. The air hostess who helped me by getting me warm water again and again because it just wouldn't reach the right temperature. I think back with gratitude to the other new mother with two little ones who offered me formula to try since the little one didn't seem to be eating properly.

So, you see all you need is to remember that many have been where you are. And no matter how prepped you think you are, something could go wrong, and you will just have to tide out the bad phase.

Prepare Uniquely for Distractions

It goes without saying you will carry some new toys, books, crafts etc. But let's face it. The magic of something new fades quickly. Try not to buy any little toys before leaving to shine in front of kids' eyes. Instead, every second or third stop treat kids to souvenirs. They can explore new vistas with their new play things in hand.

My kids got bored of every single toy that we had carried with us. The only thing that did work were the gadgets, souvenirs and the best was always the art material that they created with.

In planes, looking at the map of our progress and on road trips, playing silly games we make up.

Make the Itinerary an Activity

On our trips, we pretty much kept the kids in suspense the whole trip. So, when on our road trip across USA, we told them of all the sights we would see in St. Louis. There, we told them all the fun things planned for them in Denver. The discussion of the destination becomes an activity. This had a two-pronged effect.

They got super excited and asked questions along the way. They got involved in the planning as we searched for what all we would do.

Breaks Every 2-4 Hours

Even if the kids are sitting and not asking to go to potty, take a break. Walk them around, let them explore. Yes, sometimes you will be time bound, but this sure helps them unwind. A chance to stretch their legs, have some fun running around breaks the monotony of the ride. It is a preemptive strike against boredom.

Stay Screen Free for Long Periods

The temptation to keep the kids pacified aside, be creative in staying screen free for long periods of time. Gadgets can be used when you need to catch a nap, or the kids truly get antsy/cranky.

- Classic games are I Spy, License Plate, I'm Going on a Picnic, What Am I Thinking of.
- Try to work learning into games. I love making games up on the fly. How many cars can we count? How

145

many ways can you fold a napkin?

- Another favorite is making robots, letters from things at the table at the restaurants.
- Books of course are a great way to keep busy.
- Apps like doing puzzles and drawing are great too.
- Timeless games like charades, tic tac toe etc.

Download New Shows/Apps on the Go

Every spot that had free Wi-Fi can get utilized to give the kids hope for exciting new fun to come. Make sure to keep their most loved app/show a secret for when you hit traffic or are in a waiting area.

Rare Snacks

Keep snacks they love but haven't had in a long time in a secret compartment. They relish the fact that they can enjoy rare treats on their vacations. It also becomes something they come to expect each time they travel.

Buy Souvenirs Along the Way

We buy the kids things along the route to keep them busy and they cherish them forever. Since the memory of them buying the object is now associated with the trip, it helps them get the quick joy of receiving and keeps you from lugging around tiny toys all over your trip. Trick is to keep the purchases few and far between enough.

While on Your Adventure

The below are points to remember while you are visiting family or in a new city, so you can stay safe and make the most of your trip.

Talk to Kids About Responsibility & Safety

When visiting family, we tend to get a little lax as we know the kids are in good hands but often that is when kids tend to miscalculate their radius of fun. They walk away randomly. That's how we lost my little brother in Mumbai for 4 hours when I was 14. Which is why I'm paranoid about kids getting lost.

Talk to them about the responsibility they have while traveling. Staying within sight and not exploring new places on their own *might* not help much with them wanting to run around (they are kids after all) but helps develop a mindset of awareness. Besides counting the luggage can be a time-consuming activity as the little ones keep contradicting the older ones.

Use these tips for them to stay safe -

- Write the kids' name, address and phone number and keep them in their pockets.
- Use a marker to write your number on their forearm and paint over it with nail polish. It does not fade away.
- Instruct your child to locate another mom with kids or shop owners if lost.
- Call out loudly for you by name if they get left behind.
- Not to walk away with any strangers. Stand right where they were left. (This simple tip helped us find my brother 4 hours later in a city like Mumbai.)
- Supply kids with a whistle.
- Have set emergency guidelines if an emergency occurs.
- Talk to them about unnecessary risks. Play out situations.

Understand Local Customs and Laws

Cars stop for pedestrians in some countries and not in others. You say hello in different ways. Learn now to say few basic things in the local language. You join your hands in prayers in different ways. Search why something is different than back home. An essential process to motivate kids about being aware and being respectful of different cultures.

Include Strangers into the Trip

Strangers are after all friends we haven't met yet! My kids and I love people watching and talking to strangers. Simple conversations lead to enriched experiences as we talk about life or the city we are in. Kids learn to listen to different people and their view points. Remember to stay safe though.

Ensure the little ones know not to talk about your home, routine life or destination.

Don't Make the Trip Only About Your Child

Yes, we want the children to have fun. But kids need to know that parents too are on a break. While in Vegas for two days I told the kids, "Yesterday was your day of fun. Today is mom dad's day to do big people things like sightseeing and exploring food. You just have to tag along. It will take a lot of patience, just like we were standing yesterday while you did the rides. "

We all ended up having a good time anyway but knowing that the day was not going to have any kiddie stuff gave them the opportunity to explore with the grownups with an open mindset.

Even on our India trip when someone asks if the kids would like to visit amusement parks, I respond negatively since that is something we do enough of back home in the States.

Explore Local Treasures

Which brings me to how important it is for kids to do new or local things like museums, scenic locations, foods etc. even repeatedly when you visit family. My memories of visiting the Scindia Fort in Gwalior every summer when visiting my grandparents or the Amer Fort in Jaipur when we toured Rajasthan will forever be etched in memory. As do my kids reminisce about our cross-country road trip and the many places we visited.

Bonus Mindset Trip –

As I wondered about how the kids would react to being on the road for two days, after our first 4 hours of drive, my husband reminded me." Kids are resilient. Remember that all year round, your life revolves around them. If they do get antsy or cranky, it's okay. It's a phase and it shall pass. They will learn a lot from the experience."

And they did!

So, pack up and go plan that trip you were meaning to. Meet the family or experience a new city. It's so worth it!

19. INGRAIN RACIAL EQUALITY

Young minds do not comprehend race or cultural challenges. They are pure, simple. But as they grow, they observe those around them and imbibe what they see.

Bias, like self-preservation comes naturally to human beings, especially when it's seemingly inconsequential. But once you lean into it, the behavior becomes a habit. Since it's easy to conform to what is comfortable, known.

You don't have to take the trouble of wondering how to be or if someone is looking at you differently. You feel naturally accepted.

I have spent a lifetime scorned by the fact that language was a barrier for me growing up. Preventing me from feeling *part of the conversation.* This was before I accepted that my varied background provides me with instant rapport with most people.

When I hear someone cribbing that another culture is talking in their own language alienating those around them, I smile bringing up the fact that every single culture does this. Whether you are from the same city or speak the same language, you tend to drone on about things that others standing around you might have no idea about. The natural switch that people make towards their own kind is so inbuilt that they themselves are helpless against it.

150

There does exist racial bias or disparity in treatment by different races towards each other. My experience is limited heated conversations overheard and having to clear out of playgrounds when Arab kids came to play, for they were notorious for being careless around little kids.

That and people constantly looking to judge you. I may never understand the mentality behind it, but I fear the consequences of continued disparity.

For my children. In their future. With the way the world has been lately and the natural order of history repeating itself, I am terrified that there may be a time soon that the question of race might become very integral to living. But as history has shown us, for every point when there has been a wave of injustice against a race there have been those standing tall against it. Thankfully, for every internet emboldened hater, there are people willing to stand and say, "Love all. Stand together. "

I take heart from those that I am privileged to know for they constantly try to foster early within their children a desire to accept all. In a world where everyone is quick to take offence, we need to ensure our children practice tolerance, respect and empathy.

Talking to Kids About Race

Monkey see, monkey do.

Children don't really *see* color till they shown. My son till recently didn't comprehend cultural differences. He didn't understand why some people are vegetarian and others eat meat but accepted it at face value. Till a child remarked during lunch time how horrible it was that my son was a non-vegetarian. That is when I had to talk to him about why different people have different reasons for choosing different ways of living. How it is inappropriate to comment on others' choices. Instead we should just accept them. If curious, ask them why they choose to do so but never, ever try to influence their choice forcefully.

If you happen to see children passing racial or judgmental remarks, it is because someone in their environment has been doing the same.

On the other hand, I also know of kids who already are talking about the importance of standing up for injustices like school shootings and racial differences. That is again because their parents have experienced firsthand the unfortunate face of humanity and made their children aware of it early.

I have been privileged to have not experienced too much focused bias. And that is why I was able to shield my kids from the difficult pieces of current news. As parents we chose to shield their innocence as long as possible. Slowly, we started talking a lot more in simplest terms they could grasp about cultural differences and how history shaped things to how it is today. When I was in India, we learned Indian history which was a lot more about the development of Indian civilization and the freedom struggle of Indians from the British.

In USA, however the conversations about slavery and bigotry come up earlier due to the celebration of various holidays in school. As we researched it all at home, it became pertinent that we discuss openly the real face of history.

Personal viewpoints aside, we need to let children see the world with their own eyes. There needs to be a balance between making them aware while maintaining their innocence. We need to give them a clear vision while not tainting their glasses by our personal experiences.

How do you manage it?

Open Dialogue

Do not shush your child when they ask innocently, *"Why that man is wearing that hat?"* or *"Why that lady is wearing a dot on her head?"* Answer them with what you know or find out. Or if you are the kind of person who is open to conversation, ask them to share with you why they do so. Converse about the world as they see it.

Realize Your Part in Racial Perception

It could be as simple as an offhand remark about a cultural stereotype. This does have a huge influence on your child's perception. Stereotypes exist for a reason but understanding that they do not apply to *every* person from that culture is important. Make conscious effort towards diversity. Schools, community, books, movies all should portray your acceptance of the world as it is. Visit historic museums and be open to celebrating festivals with people from different backgrounds.

Be Honest with Your Child About Bigotry and Oppression

When you feel your child can comprehend, bring home historical books about leaders who have stood up to both. Tell stories of resistance and resilience.

Help children understand the bravery it takes to counter both. Give examples in simple ways like asking someone to sit with them or holding someone's hand when no one else does. Explain to your child that struggle for acceptance by many is real and it is something we can counter with kindness and open hearts.

Stand Equally with Every Race

I cannot forget the time my mother got so thrown by a visit from my American neighbor that she got tongue tied.

Many cultures tend to associate fairer skin with superiority. They fear offending them with their actions and tend to be more submissive to them. This unfortunately breeds a mentality of disparity within children. That they are lesser than.

Children need to understand it is not where someone comes from or how they look but how they are inside, their talent that should be appreciated, respected.

Do Not Force Your Life Choices on Others

I have seen it happen so many times. People choose a way of living and expect others to make concessions for them. Like when someone is on a dietary restriction and expect others constantly accommodate them *or* there is judgement towards how someone is living their life like when someone says "*Why do you people* ...." "(That sentence never ends well.) . Both are equally wrong.

With children, it begins with the simplest, "No, you didn't. "A child says something farfetched and another kid will counter it with "That's not right or No, you didn't." and they get into a vicious circle of trying to prove each other wrong. It is important for kids to learn early that people can be allowed to just be(when it is not harmful). They do not have to break the bubble of child who believes in Santa or that they are a super hero out to save the world! Being open to other's view points is a big part of acceptance.

Recognize Your Point of Privilege

If you have *not* experienced bias on the base of skin color, race, cultural practices, etc. you stand in a position of privilege. Not just bias. Violence, poverty, assault etc., are all a huge factor in the vantage point you hold in the perception you have to any given situation. It is important to recognize it for it is only then that you make a conscience effort to find ways to impart empathy within your children.

One can only empathize with those who think differently, if they try to tilt their perspective to view it from another angle.

Understand the Worth of Everything

This may seem weird, but I have seen kids who have no value for things and consequently lesser value of people who own them. A favorite toy of a friend thrown around, furniture being climbed upon is nothing but disrespect of the person who owns it. Caring for others' stuff goes a long way in respecting boundaries.

Listen, Not Just with Ears

Kids have a great sensitivity towards the mood of those around them. With social media and video games, listening with your ears and eyes has become a skill that needs to be re-honed. With the short attention spans we have these days, it is crucial that we teach kids to let others voice their opinion and listen with open hearts. To observe when someone is visibly uncomfortable or hurt by their actions or words. A wonderful exercise for this is after kids have had play dates. To discuss when they negated a friend callously or hurt feelings without meaning to.

Help in Every Way Possible

Encourage your little ones to help their friends however they can. Send an encouraging note to a sad friend, share, hug a friend who misses their mom, telling parents when a child is hurt, standing up for someone when others are being mean. Lending a shoulder is the surest way to encourage humility and empathy.

Kindness in karma is like energy. Never lost. Have faith that it goes around in a circle.

Acknowledge All People

One of the reasons I so love living in Richmond is most people wish you a good day, smile at you or are kind to children. Teach your children to say hello and acknowledge everyone they meet. It is the simplest way to accept the existence of another being and encourages inclusion early on.

Let little ones know that though people might look different, we are all the same inside. **RaisingWorldChildren.com**, is this global endeavor for parents to introduce children to different viewpoints from around the world.

Keep the Conversation Going. Make these empowering talks not a one off but a constant conversation. A part of your family.

20. RAISE WORLD CHILDREN

He came from preschool, placed his hand next to mine and asked, "Why is everyone in my class a different color than me?"

I was left staring. Recovering quickly, I questioned him, "Why do you ask?"

"We were doing this in class and one kid told me my skin is a different color than the rest." My son was 4. The things little kids think up is astounding!

"Did you notice anything else they have in common?", I questioned.

"Many of them have blue eyes, yellow hair while I have black."

This led to a few weeks of nightly book readings about different skin, hair and eye colors. We discussed the scientific reasons for it and about how some people look completely different from us. How we all look slightly or very different but are the same inside. About how his sister is a girl and has skin a shade lighter than him but has eyes, ears, nose and functioning organs just as him. How people sometimes do not understand different looking people and how it is important to always remember to have love in our hearts for everyone. To respect one another.

I prayed that if it was ever a serious issue, he would have the answer and heart to stand tall.

The question, "Where are you from?", has always caused me angst. My stuttered and long-winded response is hilarious even to me, as I go into the various places in India my heritage is derived from while my formative years were spent in Kuwait. "You look like a Bengali", is something I often heard from Indians since I was little. Not having met any Bengalis till recently, I wondered what that meant.

Going over every aspect of my life feels important though, for I noticed early that people warm up to a person from their state/language/heritage quickly. While it takes others a while before they can figure out what kind of person you are before they can relate to you. Isn't it ironic how people lament about how others pay more heed to people from their own culture, while doing the same themselves?

I thought it might be easier for my American born children since they can reply Richmond, Virginia. I have come to realize though; a time will come when they too will need to add *"but my parents are from India. My dad is from Lucknow raised in Gujarat. My mom was raised in Kuwait. We are Rajput by heritage."* To establish their place in the society they live in. And this will always be a requirement of being a part of the world.

To be able to identify your roots before standing tall as who you are now.

We never discussed being different, my parents and me. The significance of one's race and heritage in a person's placement in society since they were always surrounded by Indians who were expats as well. Before the Gulf war, everyone we knew spoke Hindi and stayed united in Kuwait through that thread. But I feel the extreme need to do so.

For after the Gulf war, I realized very soon if you are not comfortable in your being, without the labels, you will often find people who are willing to alter your perception, place you in a box of their choosing. For them, we were, "Those people who used live outside India." Only when they learned that we were Rajput from Gwalior would heads shake in harmony.

That is why reading, traveling, exploring and diverse conversations are useful in helping children understand and not let others' skewed perception get to them.

Knowing who you are within, keeps you rooted when the outside brings its winds of change.

It is also why we all need to begin conversations early to help kids understand themselves, the evolving world we live in and their heritage better. To enable them to make well thought out decisions better.

Raising them with an empowered mindset to rise higher when someone else goes low.

I was so disappointed when my son told me, "Some kids at school make fun of my name. They kept asking me to sing, sang some songs and then laughed." Heart pulsating, I responded calmly, "People sometimes make fun of things they don't understand."

"Yeah. I told them what my name means (Lion) but they kept laughing. "Curious, I pushed," Then.... what did you do? Ideally you have three choices. You let it go and walk away, you laugh with them or you tell them how it feels. "

"Even if they aren't respecting me, I should respect them. So, I just let it go." My eyes welled up, heart filled with pride.

It is on these days that I know that I am on the right path to raising worldly children.

***

My children and I miss out on a lot of the joys of being close to family and the little things that make our heritage special. I cannot relate when my friends wax eloquent about how much fun they had as children in India, celebrating Diwali with all the aplomb or how wonderfully they connect with their cousins back home.

I used to feel like the "Girl from nowhere." Not Indian enough and certainly not Kuwaiti by birth right. Not foreign enough then, and certainly not foreign enough here.

A few years ago, someone said to me, candidly. "You can hardly consider yourself an Indian. You haven't stayed there at all." It hurt. A lot. But eventually I accepted the truth to it. For me Kuwait will always be home. A country I may never go back to.

That does not mean I am not rooted in our Indian heritage. For my mother always ensured every festival was celebrated in grandness. Our home was the hub of celebrations and she was exemplary in her zest for life. We never had to depend on family by relations to make something unique. We just did it ourselves, with a diverse group of friends. We had our own traditions with said friends, people who we could always count on. Many of whom we will always remain connected to by heart.

Which is why I consciously incorporate every celebration I have experienced into my children's lives. Be it Christmas or Onam or Lohri or Eid.

We are not multicultural because of our religion or race or place. We are multicultural through our experiences.

I have slowly realized, I'm not the Girl from Nowhere because I belong everywhere. Every place I have been, person I have met, experience is a part of me. And a piece of me remains there too.

This is true for people everywhere. Now when someone asks me where am from, I feel happy in answering for I'm sure to connect with them in some way.

I'm a global child who has grown up to be a mother of global children.

I have been in US for 11 years now. The longest I have lived in a country. *Now, this is home for us.* I constantly emphasize that my children are not half of anything but as American as they are Indian, with a little bit of Kuwait thrown in too. It is important for them to have pride and more importantly respect for every part that makes them who they are.

In truth, I find myself learning more with my children than ever before. I am very aware that I have a great responsibility on my shoulders. Teaching our culture doesn't mean negating all others. For I am not raising just an Indian, Hindu, Rajput or American. I am raising world children who need to better comprehend and accept the differences of the people surrounding them. This only helps them understand who they themselves are and want to become!

I teach them with all my heart, that every part of them and their life is a source of celebration. For them and me. And this applies not only to my own but to every child our lives as adults touch. We all need to be aware that every choice we make helps raise world children everywhere. The karmic effect of our actions reaches far.

It is our solemn duty to enrich the lives of every child when we can, with all our experiences and lead them by example into an empowered mindset. To share with them our own identity, and all that makes us special, so they can better understand the world around them.

If you are reading this, know that your child is an amalgamation of all that's around them. Help them understand their inner self better.

- Accept that there are things about your culture that your child may not identify with. Give them time to develop that love.
- Take the time to understand your child and how to better strengthen their mindset.
- Start early with teaching them life lessons that will empower them to be of strong character.
- Let your child acknowledge the differences in cultures in their home country and the one they live in with an open mind.
- Do not belittle the country that has a special place in your child's heart.
- Find ways to incorporate new traditions into your culture.
- Make a conscious effort to consume diverse content through books, content and conversation even.
- Explore the world as much as possible. If you do not fly, take the train or car. But travel.
- Encourage curiosity within your kids about people.
- Keep an open dialogue about traditions vs today's cultures. Be open to change.
- Listen and respect your child's viewpoints.
- Let your child explore every facet of their being.
- Be the adult you want your child to become.

- Be willing to be proven wrong, when conversing with others.

Most importantly, do not expect the worst for your child. Those comments about, "Oh! When they will be a teenager, they are bound to be stuck to a video game or slam doors." are counterproductive to your mindset. Have faith in your parenting and the values you impart to them. Do not let fear of any kind cripple your parenting or your life choices. Be strong in your actions and a good example for the children around you to follow.

Life is full of unchartered territory. An adventure we never thought we would take, making decisions we constantly thought were beyond our reasoning. Make the journey with confidence, empowered in the knowledge of being sure of your self and that you are making the best decision you can with the knowledge you have with you now.

Accepting yourself as a person and parent, is the first step to raising children empowered. Only then can you raise a generation that knows how to thrive.

After all, we are all raising world children …

ABOUT AUTHOR

Aditi Wardhan Singh, Virginia based mom of two is a Computer Engineer turned author who focuses on raising awareness about cultural sensitivity and empowerment in a multicultural world. She writes heartwarming, slice of life stories for several large publications. Featured on NBC12 news and the CBS6 show Virginia This Morning, she encourages raising children rooted within. She has also co-authored the best-selling anthology 'When You're DONE Expecting'. Her initiative, the RaisingWorldChildren.com magazine has brought diverse voices around the world together to talk about the synergy of today's cultures with world heritage and how it affects parenting and thus, our children.

The girl from nowhere is how she saw herself till she realized how her varied background has positively influenced her parenting skills and thus her children. This book brings forth a lifetime of experiences of a global child and every day observations of those raising global children.

You can find more of her writings and parenting advice on – aditi.ws. You can email the RWC-Team at contact@raisingworldchildren.com. Don't forget to grab your free resources for multicultural parenting and empowerment from the RaisingWorldChildren.com website.

CPSIA information can be obtained
at www.ICGtesting.com
Printed in the USA
LVHW081923230622
721978LV00010B/602

9 781733 564908